Anxiety In Relationship

The Easiest Way to Eliminate Fear of Abandonment, Insecurity, Negative Thinking and Jealousy to Overcome Couple Conflicts and Improve Communication Between Partners.

Logan Bennett

Table of Contents

INTRODUCTION

B eing anxious is an integral part of what being human entails. Sometimes we are worried about those facets of our lives that we most care for: our health; our ability to clothe and support ourselves and our family; and our capacity to be linked and respected by others. Anxiety allows us to wake up in the morning intensively motivated to abandon our comfort zone.

Anxiety is a mental condition that can work for us as well as against us. It's something that we all share in common, but where we also vary is how we interpret these feelings of anticipation and how we react to it. Our situations in life, our culture and our attitudes can all be variables such that the thrilling rollercoaster experience of one person can leave another person in abject anxiety. Feeling anxious isn't a symptom of disappointment, and there are occasions when it's necessary to ask people around us or practitioners for support. However, as we come to a deeper understanding of anxiety, there is more we should do as people and take action to reduce its control on us and to learn to accept our full range of feelings without allowing it to overtake us.

Chapter 1

UNDERSTANDING ANXIETY

At a certain point in our lives, everyone has feelings of anxiety, whether it's about planning for a work interview, meeting a partner's relatives for the first time, or the possibility of parenthood. Although we equate anxiety with changes in our emotional state, possibly perceived as distress or discomfort, and physical signs such as elevated heart rate and adrenaline, we do recognize that this is likely to affect us only briefly once the cause of our anxiety has passed or we have learned to cope. Thus, anxiety is one of a number of feelings that have the beneficial purpose of alerting us to things we may need to think about: potentially dangerous things.

More specifically, these emotions help us identify and respond to possible challenges in an effective manner, either by quickening our reflexes or concentrating our attention on them. Anxiety, like fear, is a common feeling simply because it is part of the nature of everyone and we consider it as an integral component of our existence. However, it is also a psychological, physiological and behavioral condition that we share with animals when faced with a danger to their well-being or survival. Fear increases the anxiety, anticipation and neurobiological function of the body, which activates particular patterns of actions, intended to help us deal with an unfavorable or unpredictable circumstance.

ANXIETY AND MODERNITY

While it is the most prevalent symptom of mental illness in virtually every nation in the world, fear is still viewed as an invention of modern Western societies; for example, Norman Mailer claimed that "the normal role of man in the twentieth century is anxiety." In the first part of the twentieth century, the idea of anxiety per se was first taken as a psychological and psychoanalytical term. Freud was a leading figure in Western thinking's creation of anxiety which he thought of as a state of inner distress from which human beings are compelled to escape.

At the most fundamental level, anxiety is a warning to the ego (the personality component that interacts with reality) that something incredibly terrible is going to happen and that a defensive mechanism needs to be deployed in response. Freud saw this as deriving from the emotional helplessness of a child, which is a consequence of their biological impotence. Human beings learn to deal with anxiety caused by "actual" threats, such as fear of being attacked by a dog, either by avoiding circumstances likely to contain the threat or by actively eliminating it. Freud's typology also involved neurotic anxiety resulting from an irrational apprehension that we would lose control of libidinal desires, contributing to immoral actions and social insecurity emerging from a fear of breaking our own spiritual or cultural rules. Moral fear is manifesting itself as remorse or embarrassment, he said. Therefore, the goal of psychoanalysis is to strengthen the ego's desire to find ways to deal with fear such as "denial," "rationalization," "regression" (to a childhood state) or "projection." In the existentialist philosophical tradition, "angst" from the German word for anxiety is perceived to be a depressive emotion arising from the perception of human independence and obligation in an environment where anxiety occurs.

Anxiety conditions such as nausea, phobias and repetitive habits may be caused by unpleasant experiences, intense fear of particular things, exposure to certain circumstances or physical environments, or a constant worry that something terrible will happen in the future. A distinguishing trait of anxiety disorders is the severity and intrusiveness of psychiatric signs, such as irritability, attention problems and depression. Several may experience physical symptoms such as heart palpitations, nausea, anxiety and discomfort, slow and fast breathing, dizziness, fainting, indigestion, stomach aches, vomiting and diarrhea; in acute situations, patients have mentioned how it felt as if they were dying. The lives of people with the most extreme symptoms of anxiety may be completely consumed by their illness, suggesting that they find it difficult to relax or attain normal sleep habits, get trapped in repetitive ways of thought that hinder their ability to sustain desired behaviors, keep a job or retain personal relationships

Scott Stossel, author of *"My Age of Anxiety,"* said, "Anxiety can be both an impetus to success and an obstacle. When you're so anxious to the extent that it becomes psychologically and physically exhausting, your performance will fail.

If you are not nervous enough, if you are not engaged and, as it is, mildly triggered by fear, then your performance always suffers." The experiences of people dealing with the most severe manifestations of anxiety allow one to think of anxiety as something more than merely a disorder needing medication and care. Whether individuals deal with their anxiety, whether they handle it and interpret it to the broader world brings anxiety beyond the domain of medicine and science and into a larger sociological and cultural sense.

There are numerous types of anxiety disorders:

Post-traumatic stress disorder (PTSD), or illness, is a psychiatric response to a particularly upsetting incident beyond the context of normal activities, such as military conflict, physical violence, or a natural disaster. The signs typically include fatigue,

4

fear, hallucinations, persistent dreams, and avoiding circumstances that may cause the event's memory. One analysis of U.K. military forces deployed to Afghanistan showed that 2.7 percent of 1,431 participants were identified as likely to have PTSD, while a UK adult household survey reported a prevalence of 2.6 percent among men and 3.3 percent among women. Several studies analyzing asylum seekers and refugees' health problems have found that PTSD rates can be as much as 10-fold higher than the general age-group population (Fazel et al., 2005). Several stressors have been described as adversely impacting mental health, particularly those that occurred pre-migration, such as violence, painful starvation and incarceration, but also post-migration causes such as persecution, abuse, suffering and slow asylum decision taking (McColl et al., 2008). One study of female asylum seekers in Scotland and Belgium showed 57 percent over the PTSD symptomatology cut-off level

Obsessive-Compulsive Disorder (OCD) affects about 2-3 percent of the population and is characterized by involuntary, disruptive, recurring or repeated emotions, impulses, perceptions, sensations (obsessions) or actions that make the patient feel forced to do something (compulsions) to get rid of obsessive thinking. This only offers brief relaxation and can cause significant distress not following the repetitive routines. OCD rates in a condition can be moderate to severe anywhere, but where they are extreme and left unchecked, they will destroy the capacity of an individual to perform at work, at school, or even live a stable home life.

Generalized Anxiety Disorder: The main characteristic of generalized anxiety disorder is a continuous and persistent state of concern for various events, which is excessive in intensity, duration or frequency compared to the actual circumstances, which instead represent events feared by the subject. Anxiety is defined as "generalized" because it is not limited to certain situations, but, on the contrary, concerns a lot of events and situations. Not being associated with specific circumstances, this state is difficult to control for those who experience it and is present in the subject for most of the time for at least six months.

Excessive worries are accompanied by at least three of the following symptoms:

1. Restlessness (i.e. restless legs syndrome/restlessness);

2. Easily tired;

3. Difficulty concentrating or memory lapses;

4. Irritability;

5. Muscle tension, sometimes painful tense muscles;

6. Disturbed sleep (difficulty falling asleep or maintaining sleep, waking up with little rest).

Those who feel muscle tension may also experience tremors, aches or muscle contracts. Many people who suffer from this disorder also have somatic symptoms such as dry mouth, sticky hands, sweating, chills, nausea, diarrhea, difficulty swallowing and a lump in the throat. The worries of Generalized Anxiety Disorder have specific characteristics: for example, they are numerous, they succeed each other quickly (at the end of one there is another immediately), they are accompanied by emotions of alarm, anxiety and nervousness, they are concerned about catastrophic events futures with a low real probability of happening, reduce the ability to think clearly, are very difficult to control. Some studies have shown that those with this disorder can spend more than half the time they are awake to worry about events that do not occur. Often the person, after the missed "misfortune," recognizes his concern as excessive and disproportionate. Many concerns relate to everyday events and situations, for example, the person spends a lot of time worrying about possible misfortunes, failures or negative judgments, they can be concerned about family members, social relationships, work or school, illnesses, money and finances in general. The most common issues among people affected by the disorder are problems that may arise in the future, perfectionism and fear of failure, fear of being judged negatively by others.

To summarize, therefore, the characteristic concerns of Generalized Anxiety Disorder mostly concern events far away in time, very unlikely to actually happen, moreover the anxiety you feel is not "useful" to implement behaviors that would actually reduce the danger that is feared. Other important and typical aspects of this disorder consist on the one hand, in the fact that often the people who suffer from it are worried about having concerns, which are expressed in thoughts of "….I will not be able to control this concern;... I will never stop worrying;....I'll be sick or mad if I keep worrying like that. " The worries or anxiety about their own concerns, therefore, give rise to a vicious circle that continues to aggravate the symptoms and difficulties of daily life, inevitably affecting and influencing the mood and disposition of the person affected by this disorder. On the other hand, other people with Generalized Anxiety Disorder believe that worries can somehow have a "protective" function with respect to what they fear, that is, they tend to believe that worrying serves to prevent what is feared, for example with phrases like "... if I worry about the worst, I will be more prepared to face it...", "... if I stop worrying and something bad happens, I would feel responsible...", "... if I continue to worry, sooner or later I will know what it is better to do... ", " ... worries help me keep my anxiety under control..." Such beliefs are rarely confirmed and tested, so the person continues to worry. Starting from a concern and the related anxiety, therefore, chains of negative thoughts called ruminations are activated, which maintain and increase the initial state.

RELATIONSHIP ANXIETY:

Relationship anxiety refers to those negative emotions and concerns of doubt, worry and uncertainty about a relationship, even if all things are going on smoothly.

Is anxiety over relationships normal? Yes and no! "Relationship anxiety is incredibly common," says a psychotherapist who supports couples with relationship problems. Some individuals develop relationship anxiety at the onset of their togetherness but once they realize that their partner has an equal interest in them, it fades away. Sometimes, however, such feelings will also crop up in a long-term committed relationship.

Over time, relationship anxiety may lead to lack of energy, depression, mental discomfort, stomach pain and other physical problems. In the next chapter, we will talk more about this overwhelming phenomenon.

Chapter 2

RELATIONSHIP ANXIETY

L ove is a complex phenomenon. It may be our justification for living as well as our source of misery. It's a sweet, fundamental feeling that can turn lovers to haters and admirers to killers. For some other people, however, love is a double-edged knife that triggers something else: relationships anxiety

What exactly is relationship anxiety?

That's a kind of anxiety about romantic relationships. Instead of being happy, one continually doubts the strength and reality of love. According to Karla Ivankovich, Ph.D., a behavioral psychologist in Chicago, it's "when one or more parties in the relationship spend more time worrying about a relationship than contributing toward the relationship itself."

Though sometimes, it is natural to ask questions in relationships. So, if it's natural to have thoughts about each other's commitment in a relationship, how can you be so confident that relationship anxiety is not what you are experiencing?

SIGNS OF RELATIONSHIP ANXIETY

1) You can't help but overanalyze all time

Look, here's the thing: It's not always wrong to be cynical or critical. The ability to think deeply before investing in something really lets you distinguish facts from fiction — what is true and what is a pure illusion.

What's the problem, then? Okay, there is a problem when you never appear to be contented with the answers you receive, even though every piece of detail has already been provided after several times of cross-examination.

A good illustration is where the over-thinker tries to create situations in their own head, and they focus their decisions around things that have not yet occurred. Consider this: you're on a date. You give a good first impression with the way you are well dressed. Then while both of you are eating, you ask your guy if he had a girlfriend. Your date says "yes" – and at this point, your eyebrows are lifted. You begin to ask a battalion of questions. How did you break up? Was cheating involved? Are you people still talking? You are already getting anxious in a relationship that is yet to really start.

2) You're scared of being in a serious relationship.

How long do you think it's going to take two people to be serious about it?

For some, after the third date, this should be possible. Some people may take weeks. Others, months, years. The period depends on how well the other person has come to know you.

If you have concerns about relationships, here is your answer: "No." No matter the extent to which you are really in love with someone, you cannot commit to a relationship.

Why? There's the deep-seated doubt in the back of your mind: that you're eventually going to be alone — that you're setting yourself up again for betrayal and frustration.

After all, love will make one feel insecure according to Lisa Firestone in Psychology Today: "Letting ourselves fall in love means taking a great chance. We put a great deal of trust in another person, encouraging them to influence us whatever makes us feel insecure and weak." If you can't be sure this person is the one for you, what's the point of getting serious?

You think it makes common sense: "If you don't commit, you don't get hurt." But that's the impression that you get from anxiety about relationships.

That is what really happens: your inability to be in a serious intimate relationship keeps you from learning from experience. If you're still denying a new chance of happiness, how do you know true love, which in effect lets you get rid of relationship anxiety?

3) You develop a bad temper

Do you know what makes anxiety in relationships awful? There are many explanations for this, but this one is a big factor: not only do you harm yourself but also the ones you love dearly — even if they don't deserve it.

No matter how much love and admiration they show, you can't help but make them feel awful.

Why are you so quick to get angry? It's because you never have time for your mind to recover from your gloomy thoughts. You know this is unfair, but the fear of losing the one you love threatens to spoil your mood. In other words, you become so emotionally drained that a small annoyance is what it takes for you to go berserk.

When your partner comes home late due to work or training, you think it's the end of the world — that they don't care for you anymore. When within a day, they refuse to answer your call, you'll yell and accuse them of cheating or being an ungrateful partner.

Anxiety in relationships tricks you into believing things will all go according to schedule. Instead of being practical, you speak only in perfect terms. When your partner says something or does something that does not meet your strong standards, you believe your relationship is compromised.

Also, if you're feeling bad you begin to speak rashly — or even beat your lover. They can forgive you but remember – there's going to be a day when your wife gets fed up with your boiling temper. They are going to leave, and you are going to experience more relationship anxiety.

4) You're too attached to your partner

Relationship anxiety does not only generate anger, it also makes you needy and dependent. You are always suspicious. You're afraid that just a few minutes of silence will turn into a traumatic separation between you two. That's impossible to happen but the reverse is what your imagination suggests.

Below are several instances that could suggest that you have become too responsive to signals that your spouse may leave you:

- Responding to texts as quickly as possible and hoping for immediate responses

- Going out of your way simply to have lunch or dinner with your spouse

- Saying" I love you "at least every 15 minutes because you're afraid they're going to leave you. Yet doing it all the time can be very distracting — to the point that it makes the love gestures seem less sincere.

5) You're always going the extra mile to satisfy your partner

Love is about giving your time and energy to someone else. After all, when you go out of your way to prepare a surprise dinner or visit your lover at work, isn't it romantic?

But if you have anxiety about a relationship, it can turn into a terrible thing.

Why? Well, because you're so scared that your partner may lose interest in you, and you are now doing whatever you can to maintain an ideal self-image.

Even if it's clear that you love your partner with a single gesture, you don't think it is enough. Your lover may be happy with you, but you don't believe so.

Again, everything is in your mind, but it is enough to affect the reality.

You place all your attention on the relationship instead of balancing things like career, love and family. You don't have time to pursue your hobbies and interests any longer. You no longer even spend time with friends. It is all about having your lover impressed.

If you're trying too hard to please your partner, then you might want to have an honest conversation with your partner to reassure yourself how they feel, says Susan Krauss Ph.D. in Psychology Today: "Debating your emotions, rather than having to act on them, will not only gently remind you that your partner really cares about you — it will also assist your spouse to gain some insight into what you're doing.

6) You Lose Faith

In some situations, people who suffer a lot of anxiety in a relationship feel like this. Research also shows predictably that people with poor self-esteem have more anxiety in relationships.

Partners need to work together in a manner that demonstrates they are comfortable in the compromise and friendship in order to be in a stable relationship that is full of confidence and happiness.

If you're lacking trust and afraid your partner will see how terrified you are of losing them or getting hurt, it could turn the pot the wrong way. We often dread what may be in front of us, rather than what is right in front of us. What is normally right before us is proof that the partnership is going well, but we believe that we are not deserving of it.

7) You're trying to regulate everything

When you're worried about your relationship, you may find yourself doing whatever you can to make sure things look exactly like this, because they're just like that. Perfection is a daunting aim for people to achieve, but for certain people it is not necessarily apparent that it is unattainable.

When you're trying to keep your ducks in a row and you don't have to confront reality, that may have the opposite impact and lead you to feel much more depressed than if the entire situation were to fall apart. According to relationship psychologist Orly Kataz in *Bustle*, managing issues helps to minimize ambiguity: "Typically as problems occur, the fear arises from confusion and cannot foresee or handle the outcome...In their effort to take over and alleviate ambiguity and distress, the [anxious person] is viewed as manipulating, intimidating, and challenging."

If fear is a part of your friendship, or you believe it is, you can find that in your life you conceal things from events, and conceal things from people. You may not know how much at first you're pushing back, but over time, you'll see how you're getting insecure about the relationship you're in, and not the other way around.

A successful litmus check is to take stock of your other relationships and decide whether you are giving yourself the pain you hear. When your relationships are broken with friends, relatives, and colleagues, it may be a clear sign that you are the source of your tension and unhappiness.

Don't panic because you're making this journey because it means you can turn things upside down. Your fear may affect you, according to *Bustle*: "Your fear may affect you but it's not who you are as a human. It will affect your partnership, but it doesn't mean that you can't have one, or that in the future you and your wife won't be happier."

Chapter 3

UNDERSTANDING JEALOUSY

Jealousy can be described as being diligent in preserving or protecting things. Ordinarily, jealousy is bad, but it's natural to want to defend the ones we love, particularly when we see that they are being targeted by our rivals. But there is a distinction between feeling jealous and expressing dangerous jealousy.

Natural jealousy is a reaction that comes on in a moment, one that we can normally ignore on our own. As anxiety in our relationships is rife, jealousy will easily become fear and obsession, threatening to ruin the very relationship that we are most afraid to lose.

No one wants to be jealous. Yet jealousy is an inherent feeling that almost any one of us will feel. The trouble with jealousy is not when it comes from time to time, but what it does to us when we can't control it. It can be disturbing to see what happens when we allow our jealousy to overtake us or shape the way we feel about ourselves and the world around us. That's why knowing where our jealousy truly comes from and learning how to deal with it in a safe, constructive way is the secret to success in many areas of our lives, from our interpersonal relationships to our jobs to our personal goals.

A lot of us must have felt it at one time or another. It could be a slight irritation or a fiery fire inside you, consuming you and making you feel like you could burst. Although it's a normal emotional reaction when a person feels threatened, jealousy is one of the biggest destroyers of relationships. Jealousy can range from feeling angry that your husband is admiring another woman, or that your wife is staring at another man, to imagining things that aren't there. Either way, jealousy will have a detrimental effect on your relationship.

WHAT IS JEALOUSY?

While feeling jealous is something we can all recall, the emotion is also mistaken with envy. Envy and jealousy though, are very distinct. Envy is a reaction to personal lack and an indecent desire for what is in possession of someone else. You may be envious of somebody's attractive features, or their delightful house, etc. Jealousy, however, happens when you are afraid that somebody intends to take what's yours. For instance, your better half is relating with a beautiful co-worker, you may begin to feel jealous.

The mildest jealousy is considered an intuitive reaction that makes us need to shield what we know is our own. Nevertheless, unlike just being defensive, jealous emotions will easily balloon into destructive actions and lead us to behave in selfish and manipulating ways. This may also lead one to believe that there are incidents that are not true, such as seeing a brief conversation as the symbol of adultery or working late as keeping a secret relationship.

Instinctual or not, jealousy has nothing good to offer. Those who struggle with manipulating, competitive feelings frequently often deal with deeper problems. Usually, unchecked jealous activity is a symptom of one or more of the following

- Anxiety

- Apprehension

- Poor confidence

Knowing the root of behavior will permit you to be able to control it. Either of those three, or their mixture, will not only cause a sense of envy to manifest in disruptive behavior but will also generate certain issues in the life of an individual

WHY DO PEOPLE GET JEALOUS?

Researches have revealed that expanded jealousy is connected to decreased confidence. "Most of us are still oblivious of the underlying guilt that resides inside us, as it is too natural to speak of self-critical thoughts about ourselves. But the guilt in our history will have a huge effect on the degree to which we feel insecure and confused in the present," said Dr. Lisa Firestone, author of *"Conquer The Vital Inner Spirit."* As Dr. Robert Firestone and her father describe it, "powerful inner voice" is a form of negative self-talk. It perpetuates negative thoughts and feelings, causing us to compare, assess and analyze ourselves (and often others) with considerable scrutiny. This is one of the reasons that learning how to deal with jealousy is so important.

This voice will intensify our feelings of jealousy by flooding our heads with negative and provocative remarks. In reality, what our vital inner voice tells us about our condition is often more difficult to cope with than the situation itself. Our partner's rejection or deception is traumatic, but what really kills us is all the horrible thoughts that our vital inner voice tells us about ourselves after the incident. "You are such an idiot. Did you ever believe that only you should be happy? You're going to end up alone. You can never trust someone again." To illustrate how this inner enemy fuels our pessimistic emotions about envy, we're going to look more closely at two types of envy: emotional jealousy and competitive jealousy. While these two types of envy frequently intersect, understanding them individually will help us to understand how jealous emotions will affect different aspects of our lives and how we can properly cope with envy.

ROMANTIC JEALOUSY

It's a common fact that marriages get better as people don't get unnecessarily jealous. The longer we will hang onto our feelings of envy and make sense of them apart from our partner, the happier we will be. Note, our envy also stems from our own fear – a sense that we are destined to be misled, harmed or rejected. Unless we cope with this feeling in ourselves, we are likely to fall prey to feelings of envy, mistrust or anxiety in any relationship, whatever the circumstances.

Such pessimistic thoughts about ourselves stem from the very early experiences of our lives. We regularly take on the sentiments that our folks or significant guardians have had towards us or towards themselves. At that point, unwittingly, we replay, reproduce, or respond to old, recognizable elements in our present connections. For starters, if we feel set out as adolescents, we might easily see our partner as rejecting us. We can prefer a partner who is more elusive or even participates in actions that will drive our partner away from us.

The degree to which we have developed self-critical attitudes as children also affects how much our critical inner voice can affect us in our adult lives, particularly in our relationships. No matter what our particular perspectives can be, to a degree we all share this inner critic. Most of us can respond to a sense that we're not going to be picked. The level to which we accept this insecurity influences how insecure we feel in a relationship.

"Are you the source of your jealousy?" Lurking beneath the hostility against our friends or questioning supposed third-party threats are also serious thoughts about ourselves. Thoughts like, *"What's he seeing in her? Can easily turn into she's so prettier/thinner/more effective than me!"* As our worst instincts materialize when we hear about a partner's affair, we still respond by directing our rage toward ourselves for being "foolish, unloved, destroyed or rejected. Like a sadistic teacher, our cruel inner voice warns us not to trust or feel too weak. It reminds us that we are unlovable and not cut out for marriage. It's the gentle whisper the plants a seed of skepticism, distrust and confusion. Why does she work late? Why does he choose his friends over me? What does she do while I'm away? How come he pays so much attention to what she says? Those of us who know how envy works know that, all too often, these feelings will gradually begin to bloom and blossom into even bigger, more intense assaults on ourselves and/or our partner. She does not want to be around you. There's got to be something else. He's lost confidence. He needs to get away from you. Who wants to listen to you? You're so dull. This jealous feeling will emerge at any stage in a relationship, from the first date to the 20th year of a marriage. In an effort to defend ourselves, we can listen to our inner critic and withdraw from being close to our partner. In the final catch 22, we still seem to get more competitive as we refrain from doing what we want. If we know at any level that we don't consider our relationship a priority or consciously follow our aim of being intimate or similar, we continue to feel more insecure and more competitive. That's why it's much more important to know how to deal with envy and not unconsciously act on envy by driving our partner farther backward.

COMPETITIVE JEALOUSY

While it can feel pointless or illogical, it is very common to desire what others have and to feel competitive. Yet how we use these emotions is really important to our sense of fulfillment and happiness. If we use these emotions to support our inner enemy, to break down ourselves or others, this is simply a negative trend of demoralizing consequences. However, if we do not let these emotions fall into the hands of our vital inner mind, we will potentially use them to understand what we desire, to be more goal-oriented, or just to be more accepting of ourselves and what affects us.

It's all right, even safe, to encourage us to think competitively. It can feel good if we just let ourselves have a momentary feeling without a decision or action plan. But whether we ruminate or twist this idea into a critique of ourselves or an assault on another human, we end up getting hurt. If we find ourselves overreacting or haunted by our thoughts of jealousy, we should do a few things.

Be aware of what is initiated. Think about the various things that cause you to feel anxious. Is there a companion who has a money related achievement? A friend who's dating someone else, huh? A co-worker who speaks her mind at a meeting?

Tell yourself what kind of vital inner voices are coming up. What kind of thoughts do these jealous emotions give rise to? Do you use these feelings of jealousy to put yourself down? Do they make you feel worthless, incompetent, inadequate and so on? Is there a trend or theme to these thoughts that you are familiar with?

Think about the broader meaning and roots of these thoughts: do you sense a strong urge to do something? Is there something you think you're going to be? What does this thing mean to you? Is it linking to your past?

When we have asked ourselves these questions, we will understand how these feelings could have more to do with unanswered problems within ourselves than with our present life or the individual to whom our envy is directed. We should show more respect for ourselves and seek to postpone the prejudices that cause us to feel insecure.

GOOD JEALOUSY VERSUS PATHOLOGICAL JEALOUSY

Occasional rivalry is normal and may keep a relationship going. But when it is extreme or excessive, it may do significant harm to a relationship. In marriages where feelings of envy are mild and sporadic, it teaches couples not to take each other for granted.

Jealousy can also inspire partners to respect each other and make a conscious effort to make sure their partner feels appreciated. Envy also heightens desires, making desire deeper and sex more passionate. In low, stable doses, envy can be a productive influence in a marriage.

But when envy is strong or irrational, it's a completely different matter. In addition, irrational or intense envy is always a warning sign of potentially unhealthy relationships. Eventually, jealous people are so confused by their feelings and contradictions that they continue to exert control over their partners. They can also resort to aggression, financial coercion, and verbal intimidation to retain power and ease or conceal their envy.

JEALOUSY RISK DYSFUNCTIONAL

Jealousy doesn't become a problem until it's over. People who are prone to extreme envy or possessiveness frequently harbor feelings of inadequacy or inferiority and have a propensity to compare themselves to others. Desire, at its heart, is a result of tension, uneasiness of not being adequate, dread of disappointment. Once it happens, it may cause one to assume that our relationship is in imminent danger, making it difficult to differentiate between normal feelings of security and unreasonable fear. In other words, it's pretty bad. But the first time we see the envy flare-up in our partner, we can see it as "good" and say, "Oh, this person must really love me!" If it is a good kind of envy, those emotions will fade away without an incident and without negatively affecting the relationship. But we need to be alert to early warning signs of unsafe behavior because it can lead to other forms of abuse.

Unhealthy partnerships often begin with minor things like a suspicious partner looking for signs of cheating. When they come up empty instead of feeling happy, they will vent their anger through a number of tactics while tearing down their self-esteem with allegations, remorse, name-calling, and threats before moving on to emotional and physical violence. Their tactics take several forms, but as their resentment increases, so does the chance to intensify. That's why it's crucial to recognize red flags early on.

WHAT UNHEALTHY JEALOUSY LOOKS LIKE

It can be easy to equate dysfunctional jealousy with passion. These are common warning signals that frequently indicate risky complications at the beginning of partnerships and escalate later on.

You are supposed to devote all the time to them. They're not only happy to see you, they're insistent. They're telling you to blow off your game, leave your buddies, or drop out of work, school, or family responsibilities because they've "never felt this way before" and "need to be next to you." They can be pouty/whiny when you don't agree because they continue to pop up everywhere you are, uninvited. They hate being away from you, and they keep in touch with you while you're not together.

Despite the fact that it might sound decent when somebody attempts to invest all their energy with you, an individual who cherishes you will understand that you need time away from a relationship. You deserve the freedom to be alone and follow other interests without being disciplined for it. A loving partner would never ask you to give up your interests, friends, careers, or events to consume your time.

You're expected to check-in. Your significant other wants to know where you are. They ask what you're doing, and who you're with. If you're gone, they're calling, texting, or messaging you via social media all the time, hoping for an instant reply, waiting on you to keep him/her up to date on your single breath when you're apart.

A stable relationship doesn't require a "check-in." Your partner shouldn't expect you to remain in regular touch while you're gone, and no one will ever insist on watching you with an app or any other device. Understanding that you're protected will be enough because if you don't, your limits won't be honored. You are your own individual, and you are entitled to live your own life.

THERE ARE RULES ON HOW YOU SHOULD TALK WITH

You know there are individuals your partner does not like you associating with; the list can incorporate exes, individuals you used to hate, the flirtatious friend, and so on. The excuses you're not allowed to talk to, and others are different: "I trust you, I just don't trust them."

Demands on who you can speak to will lead to an intimidation technique called isolation. What starts with not being able to speak to a certain person becomes the guidelines for keeping away from just about everyone they believe is vying for their love, money, or interest. Eventually, everything is out of reach when you become confined to your family alone, paving the way for loneliness and potentially, physical assault.

It's never all right to control who your partner can and can't speak to. Part of respecting someone means trusting them to make the best choices for the relationships they have. You should express your feelings in a caring, honest way, but then you must trust the judgment of your partner. If one of you can't trust the other, it might be time to move on.

They're suspicious. When you go out with your buddies, you know you're going to get a third-degree from your wife. It's the fear while you're out and they're told everyone's flirting with you. Often it only takes someone else to look at you and get mad, and then they're behaving like you're at fault and then you're blamed. You are accused of being overly nice, dressed overly provocatively, or giving people "the wrong impression." No matter how much you convince them of your faithfulness, they never trust you.

Persons in stable relationships don't put any action of their partner under the microscope. We should not continually challenge the motives of the other, or laden them with questions of suspicion. Love does not search for evidence or presume wrongdoing — insecurity does.

When there are struggles of on-going skepticism, there might be a larger underlying problem, so the arrangement won't work until it's dealt with. Relationship withers if distrust overwhelms confidence.

THEY ARE POSSESSIVE

They've given you jewelry or personal memento that they want you to wear all the time, so people think you're being taken. Then if they're not too touchy in private, they're big on public shows of affection, particularly if your ex is around. They're all over social media and insist on sharing profile pictures and status messages together. They're rude to someone they think you're going to get close to. They have made you skip parties or break plans to be with them and making comments like, "You're mine," or, "No one will ever love you like me." Films and books have a terrible habit of romanticizing this behavior; in real life, the aim of a possessive partner is not to share you with others. They work through the need for power and will seek to exploit you mentally, using gifts, over-the-top gestures, and praise to return your "belonging" to them. Their fixation will escalate to physical confrontations with others they see as rivalry, and if their behavior progresses, they won't shy away from insulting you in public if it means demonstrating their dominance; for example, they will scream at you and grab your arm to make you leave a party. For possessiveness, physical violence and alienation are not far away.

People in healthy, dedicated marriages realize that love involves allowing their significant others to have room to be their own. We let go of the need to mark their turf or scare off rivals because we trust each other.

They've have a quick temper. One minute you're looking forward to enjoying dinner at your dream place, next to your partner's making the scene because you've arrived a few minutes late. It happens very frequently, so you blame yourself for the fact that you know your friend has buttons that lead them to become angry, so it's your responsibility to not press them. You hope you could be a great girlfriend/boyfriend, but you're always fucking up, giving them a justification to blow up. Some days you feel blessed they're so gracious and always trust you, though you make too many mistakes, even though you're cautious.

If your partner's temper is easy to draw, it's not a representation of you. It necessarily means they haven't learned how to deal with confrontation, or they may use it as a way of influencing, regulating or governing you. It's not your fault, either way.

People in healthy marriages work together to settle disputes. We are committed to finding ways to work around issues without hurting or disrespecting the other party. If your reaction is always frustration, it is not your duty to continue and be a mental, verbal, or physical outlet for it. This isn't love.

THEY TRACK YOUR INTERACTIONS

Your partner tells you they're an open book and they don't want any secrets between you two. That is the reason you need passwords for your phone, email address, Twitter, SnapChat, Instagram, and any web-bascd gadget you're utilizing. They're scrolling through your messages, they're asking you about calls, they're fine-tuning your words, and they're deleting interactions they don't support, with or without your consent. Often you find that your password doesn't work or that you've been shut out of your own account. You remind yourself that this isn't a big deal; it's a small price to pay to be with them and show them that they can trust you.

Wanting your passwords isn't about love, it's about superiority and power. Your passwords are your own, and someone who demands that you offer this code does not believe you and is behaving in a regulated manner.

Good partnerships do not allow you to justify your trustworthiness, as trust does not require evidence. Also, if you don't mind sharing information, to engage in this negative behavior is to demonstrate that it's okay to invade your privacy, to open the door to other coercive behaviors along the way.

THEY'RE EMOTIONALLY SENSITIVE

You found that your partner came out hard right from the beginning, however, you thought it was on the grounds that you cherished them to such an extent. We would rather not be separated at this point. They're continually calling and reaching you and going through the entirety of your online life pages, sharing as well as posting on something, including things that are years old. They simply needed to keep you all alone, and they were quick to state, "I love you," despite the fact that they felt powerless. Discussions of "forever" come up a ton, and they consider whether they "go crazy," "pass on" or "slaughter" themselves if you two really separate. It tends to be difficult to escape from them, in light of the fact that occasionally you believe they're watching you.

Although it may be flattering to know that everyone loves us so much, there is emotional vulnerability underneath the surface. If they are too intense from the start, the same desire can turn into strenuous physical attacks, bullying, threats of self-harm, and/or abuse.

Good couples know that they can't know everything about their partner. That person wants a certain degree of freedom and liberty, which is why you can never be held responsible for the welfare of another person. Emotional pressure also creates a sense of suffocation, and if you feel that way, don't dismiss it.

WHAT JEALOUSY DOES TO YOUR RELATIONSHIP

Jealous conduct can be incredibly detrimental to your relationship. At all, a disgruntled partner is in search of reassurance that they are the only ones and that no one is a challenge to replace them. Worst of all, envy can manifest itself in oppressive and distrustful conduct, and even physical or emotional violence.

A jealous spouse can attempt to regulate their partner's acts, to verify where they are going, or to track their calls, texts or e-mails. Such conduct generates a cycle of mistrust that is unhealthful and can inevitably lead a relationship to fail.

Trust and respect are the cornerstone of every safe and successful relationship. A person dealing with envy cannot trust the person they are with or display regard for them as an entity or as a boundary.

Over time, this action would disrupt the feelings of passion and devotion that once existed. This is therefore apt to trigger repeated disputes and the need for one party to prove themselves and their integrity over and over again. This can be overwhelming and keep a partnership from developing and building a stable base.

UNDERSTAND THE REASONS FOR YOUR TRIGGERS

Shortcomings than your partner's behavior. E.g., if you have had traumatic encounters in your life, you might be susceptible to envy. It's important to speak to your friend about these interactions so that you can be conscious and accept each other's causes.

Jealousy may be motivated by a weak self-esteem or a bad self-image. When you don't feel desirable and comfortable, it can be hard to genuinely accept that your partner likes and respects you. At other times, envy can be caused by unreasonable perceptions of the relationship. Note that emotions are not the truth. Were you seeing things that aren't there? I urge my clients to challenge themselves, "Is that right? "Is this really going on? When the conclusion is no, let go of the pessimistic feelings. Recognize them before deliberately ignoring them.

Thoughts of envy may be troublesome because they affect your actions and your thoughts towards the relationship as a whole. Below are some symptoms of unhealthy jealous behavior.

- Checking your partner's phone or email without permission
- Insulting
- Saying that your spouse is not attractive to you
- Grilling your spouse about their location during the day
- Accusing your spouse of deception without proof

HOW TO DEAL WITH JEALOUSY - WHAT TO DO

- **Remember what is stirring up** – Daniel Siegel uses the word SIFT to explain how we can sift through the emotions, pictures, feelings and thoughts that occur as we focus on other things in our lives. We're meant to try and do that when we feel insecure. We should ask what kind of emotions, pictures, perceptions, and thoughts of envy give rise to. Is the present situation causing the ancient – a dysfunctional family or a long-held, pessimistic self-perception? The more we can relate these feelings or overreactions to previous events that first produced them, the better we can experience our present-day situation.

- **Calm down and remain relaxed** – no matter how angry we are, we should find opportunities to get back to ourselves and loosen up. Second, we will do so by acknowledging our feelings with compassion. Remember that no matter how powerful we are, our emotions continue to flow in waves, first constructing, then subsidizing. It is important to consider and understand our envy without acting on it. We may learn strategies to calm down before responding, for example, by taking a stroll or a series of deep breaths. It's much harder to calm down in this manner because we fail to accept or engage in the angry comments of our inner critic, and it's important to know how to question this. When we do, we will speak up for ourselves and the ones we matter about and stay honest and open to our relationship.

- **Don't move** – Our vital inner voice continues to urge us to take action that will harm us in the long run. When it spirals us into a state of envy, it may convince us to give up or stop chasing after what we want. This could drive us to self-sabotage, blow up, or threaten anyone we admire. When we're in a partnership,

30

we may be asked to freeze or lash out at our partner. When we do that, what we do is build a situation that we're scared of. We harm and weaken the feelings of love our spouses have for us, and we may bring up their own feelings of mistrust and fear. We can unconsciously allow them to become more guarded, less transparent about their emotions, thoughts and acts, which then contributes to our emotions of mistrust and envy.

- **Look for our own sense of confidence** – the only thing we can do is to feel confident and safe in ourselves. We've got to do the work of overcoming our inner enemy and pretending that we're all right, even on our own. We don't need the affection of a single person to feel that we are lovable. Human beings are full of faults and weaknesses, and no one can give us what we need 100% of the time. That's why it's so important to exercise self-compassion and strive to stand up to our own inner critic. It doesn't mean locking us off or closing ourselves out from what we want to do. It simply means to accept our lives with all our souls, while acknowledging that we are healthy enough to struggle or lose. No matter what, we will live with the feelings that emerge.

- **Keep optimistic** – A lot of people disagree on the thought of competition, but what we're talking about here isn't the goal of being the best, but a real goal of doing the best we can do. It implies feeling like ourselves and tolerating the qualities that can support us and accomplish what we need. Rather than causing the green beast to change us into beasts, we ought to urge ourselves to feel enabled, to associate with who we need to be, and to make a move that takes us closer to that. When we want respect for those around us, we need to be respectful and careful about our interactions. When we want to know the unconditional affection of our family, we must dedicate ourselves to enjoying each and every day. When we retain a commitment to act with dignity and follow our objectives, we will win the most critical fight we will face, the struggle to recognize and become our true self-separate from everyone else.

- **Chat about it** – When something like anger takes over, it's important to find the right person to speak to, and a safe way to convey what we're feeling. The ones who embrace the good side of us and help us avoid ruminating or slipping deeper into our sorrows are the sort of friends we want to talk to about our envy. We also have friends who get a bit more worked up when we bring up those things, so they may not be the right people to figure out why we get stimulated so easily. We will try to meet someone that can help us keep on track and be the sort of people we want to be. Venting to these is good as long as it's a matter of letting go of our emotional thoughts and feelings while realizing that they're distorted and unfounded. The method only succeeds because it relieves us of guilt and helps us to move on and take positive steps. If we suffer from feelings of envy, it is always very important to get the aid of a psychiatrist. This will help us make sense of our emotions and get a grip on them while behaving in a safer, more proactive way.

It is necessary to maintain a transparent, truthful relationship with our partner. When we expect that they will have their confidence and that they will have ours, we will listen to what they say without getting defensive or jumping to conclusions. This open line of communication is not about unloading our insecurities on our friend, but about encouraging us to be kind and linked, even though we feel insecure or jealous. This obviously encourages our companion to do the same thing.

There is no doubt that it takes a certain degree of moral intelligence to cope with the multiple emotions of envy. It needs the courage to confront our vital inner voice and all the complexities it creates. It always takes the courage to stand back and stop acting on our impulsive, angry responses. Also, as we cultivate this strength in ourselves, we know that we are far smarter than we believe we are. In learning how to deal with envy, we are more confident both in ourselves and in our relationships.

USING JEALOUSY POSITIVELY

Envy in a relationship may also be a very true and rational reaction to your partner's behavior. Note, in a strong enough relationship, people have high hopes about how to handle them. They deserve compassion, caring, intimacy, and reverence to be received. We expect their companion to be honest and trustworthy.

"Is that the case?" Yes, so it's important to tell your partner how you feel before your envy turns into resentment. If you bring it up, stick to the "I" words, and avoid saying something like "you still" or "you never." Talk about your thoughts about a particular situation and avoid saying something about your partner's character. Tell me what you need, not what you don't need.

"I get nervous, for starters, because I don't know where you are or who you're with when you're out. I need you to contact me to let me know." The more you talk, the better the relationship becomes. Is there a particular arrangement that leaves you uncomfortable? Are you feeling that you're being stonewalled or that your partner's behavior has changed recently?

You and your partner should be open and honest with partnerships and working relationships with each other. Transparency is going to make you feel better. When you're not aware of the limits, a reasonable rule of thumb is to ask yourself, "How would I react if I heard my wife speak to anyone else like this?" If it happens, the line is crossed.

Show each other how much you respect each other by putting your relationship above your job, your family, and your friends. You create confidence every time you do this.

By knowing what drives your emotions and respecting each other's endearing flaws, you will use envy for good.

OVERCOMING JEALOUSY AND POWER IN RELATIONSHIPS

Overcoming jealousy is like altering certain emotional reactions or behavior. It's starting with understanding. Awareness helps you to see that the myths portrayed in your head are not real. You no longer succumb to the situations that your imagination creates when you have this insight. Jealousy and rage are cognitive responses to thinking things that are not real in your head; in changing what you think, you're shifting what your mind is creating, so you can remove these damaging emotional reactions. Sometimes, even if there is a reason for the reaction, envy and rage are not helpful approaches to deal with the situation and get what we want. Trying to alter frustration or envy while you're in your feelings is like trying to steer a vehicle on the ice. Your ability to deal with the situation is significantly enhanced if you can steer clear of the danger before we get there. It includes confronting the biases that cause envy instead of attempting to suppress the emotions. To completely dissolve feelings such as frustration and envy in relationships means to shift the underlying values of confusion and the internal expectations of what the partner is doing.

Steps to finally bring an end to envy are:

- Restoring moral influence so that you can control your feelings and stop aggressive behavior.

- Switch the point of view so that you can step back from the tale on your head. It would give you a window of time to stop a negative or angry response and do something else.

- Identify the fundamental values that cause an emotional response.

- Be mindful that the assumption in your mind is not valid. It is different from "knowing" scientifically that the claims are not real.

- Gain power over your thoughts so that you can actively determine what story is on your head and what feelings you have.

There are a variety of factors that give rise to a phenomenon of envy. As such, viable approaches would have to tackle several elements of conviction, perspective, sentiment, and strength of a person. If you skip one or more of these components, you leave the door open to the return of certain negative feelings and behaviors.

By doing a few basic techniques, you will step back from the tale that your imagination is creating and refrain from emotional reactions. If you just want to change your feelings and actions, you can do it. This only requires the ability to learn useful skills. In self-mastering classes, you can consider useful techniques and activities to conquer the emotional responses of envy.

PRINCIPLE CAUSES OF JEALOUSY ARE ASSUMPTIONS THAT GENERATE FEELINGS OF CONFUSION

Feelings of poor self-esteem are centered on the assumption that we have in the internal picture of who we are. In order to remove the anxiety and poor self-esteem that have, we don't have to change, we just need to shift our confidence in the fake self-image. Although some may believe that this may be daunting, it is only hard because most may have not developed the skills required to alter their convictions. When you practice your skills, you find that it takes very little time to improve your belief. You're just going to avoid believing the story in your head. It takes more time to believe something than not to believe it.

SELF JUDGEMENT WILL INTENSIFY THE FEELING OF VULNERABILITY

It is not enough to "learn" scientifically that we are generating emotions. With this information alone, the inner judge is apt to torment us with criticism of what we are doing. The inner judge may use this knowledge to put us into an emotional downward spiral of more vulnerability. In order to create a more positive difference, you would need to develop skills to remove illusions and distorted self-images to take control over what your mind creates.

One of the moves to change behavior is to see how, in our heads, we unconsciously generate an emotion of rage or envy from pictures, values, and perceptions. This step not only encourages us to take responsibility, but it also places us in a position of control to alter our emotions.

If you're in a relationship with a jealous friend, and they expect you to change your actions to escape jealousy, they don't take responsibility. If they say something like "If you wouldn't then I wouldn't respond that way." That kind of language flags a mentality of powerlessness and an effort to regulate your actions with a relationship.

WHY THE SUBCONSCIOUS PRODUCES THE FEELINGS OF JEALOUSY AND ANGER

When you're struggling to conquer envy, you're probably already familiar with the complexities. This explanation can help to fill some holes in how the mind turns awareness into self-esteem and reinforces low self-esteem and insecurity. Such analytical insight will help you create confidence in order to consider these complexities in the time you do them. Yet if you ever want to make meaningful improvements, you need a different skill set. Knowing how you're generating your emotional feelings doesn't give you enough details on how to alter them. Much like realizing that you had a flat tire when you walked over a nail doesn't mean you know how to fix the tire.

Take for example, a man feeling self-assured. Insecurity stems from his distorted secret belief that he is "not good enough." By assuming that this fake picture is him, rather than the reality, a man causes self-rejection in his head. The mental consequence of self-denial is a feeling of indignity, vulnerability, anxiety, and unhappiness.

COMPENSATION FOR INSECURITY

In order to alleviate the anxiety created by his secret identity, he reflects on his perceived positive attributes. The man builds a more optimistic false picture of himself from these values. That is what is called the projected identity because that is how it needs to be used. The mental consequence of a good self-image is no self-denial and no feeling of indignity. There is more appreciation of himself, and he generates more love and joy. Remember that he hasn't shifted, he's just hanging on to a different vision in his head, based on the moment.

Secret identity beliefs are the causes of unhappiness, while the perceived identity activates more positive feelings. It's important to remember that both images are fake. All images are in the imagination of the man, and neither is he. He is the one that generates and responds to the pictures of his mind. In his imagination, he is not the image.

37

The subconscious of the man connects the imagined portrait with the characteristics that women are drawn to. As a consequence of the belief that women are drawn to them, consistency is always considered good. When a man gets the affection of a woman, he identifies himself with the perceived identity rather than the "not good enough" one. Strengthened trust in the perceived identity results in more self-acceptance, affection, and satisfaction in his emotional state.

This is the behavior of the man's recognition and affection that transforms his emotional state. It's not the face or the popularity of a woman that affects her emotions. Those are simply stimuli that activate the mind of the man against other values, self-acceptance, and affection.

The man's subconscious also makes the mistaken impression that he "gets him happy" or that he "uses" her to be happy. It only looks this way when he understands a woman's connection to her emotional condition. Often, a man doesn't know that she's just an emotional stimulus for his mind to show affection. He could not have developed other triggers to communicate his own approval and affection, such that he relies on a woman for a cause. When a man understands that he is just a catalyst and that his role in communicating appreciation and affection is what affects his emotional state, a man does not "use" his wife to be content.

CONTROLLING ACTIONS

The man works with a delusional perception that he is happy because of the affection and devotion of a woman. When he imagines that his attention is to someone or something other than himself, he responds with terror. Much of the fear is not about losing a girlfriend, as he may mistakenly assume. Much of the anxiety is about preventing the physical suffering that the secret identity produces in his head.

His secret identity convictions will become involved without her knowledge. His point of view about himself often moves to the understanding of this "not good enough" society. His feeling of indignity and unhappiness reflects his model of conviction and perspective.

The man is attempting to attract to monitor the focus of the woman so that the predicted image becomes successful. He's working to "disable" her "gun" to help his predicted image beliefs. It's the way he uses to stop his socially upsetting secret identity convictions. He is not conscious that the communication of affection and appreciation is the way to alter his emotional state.

RAGE AND RETALIATION FOR MANIPULATING ACTIONS

One of the ways we know early in life is to control the interest and conduct of other people through the emotion of indignation. If we were disciplined as infants, indignation always preceded the penalty. Occasionally, harsh words were enough to get us to change our actions. At the very least, when anyone was upset at us, we had their attention. Throughout this way, we learned early in life to use indignation as a method of regulating the actions of others and as a punishment for manipulating behavior. We didn't automatically unlearn this habit when we grew older.

The jealous man is using his partner's rage to get and control her affection. Anger also serves as a deterrent for causing physical distress on the victim. Through threatening a woman in anger, a woman will alter her actions in order to escape physical retribution in the future.

The use of rage by a man may not be his chosen option. But his action of frustration is the product of a distorted concept of perception. He "thinks" differently at the level of his mind, but his conduct is based on mistaken assumptions and the secret identity that activates his emotions.

THE REAL OUTCOME OF MANAGING RAGE

In his frustration, the guy has the opposite effect that he's been programmed to get as a child. A person usually has the ability to avoid the abuse of rage than a child does. The woman is going to break from him because of her propensity to resist the socially negative. Her removal would trigger his secret identity illusion that he was trying to escape. The man's belief-emotion loop is moving back to the beginning. It's physically hard.

ANALYSIS AFTER THE INCIDENT

Following an incident of resentment and rage, there is an incentive to look at and evaluate the incidents. For a jealous man, this time may also be emotionally more stressful. It is where his own decision will be at the lowest.

The man plays the action of rage and power of his mind. Nonetheless, it is now being examined from the point of view of the inner judge of his opinion. The inner judge shall carry out the review and condemn it. Specifically, the inner judge holds up the perceived identity and then points out that "he failed" to live up to the level. He can only assume, based on the perceived identity norm, that he is a loser and not good enough.

The rage event, as interpreted by the inner judge, is "proof" that he is indeed the person who fits the image of the secret identity. Acknowledging and accepting this decision results in a man feeling guilty, with feelings of remorse and humiliation. The conviction, feeling, and perception of the secret identity character is confirmed. The inner judge will not grant the man a fair trial. It's a lawyer who's there. The inner judge shall not determine the position of the belief system, the false images or the point of view.

The guy in his head is at the mercy of the powers that he has not been trained to see and deal with. With the knowledge of these powers and some practical practice, he will begin to gain control of his emotional state.

EFFORTS TO MODIFY ACTIONS MAY NOT APPEAR TO SUCCEED

The key issue in the research is that an individual is observing situations from a judgmental point of view. Judgment leads to denial. It also helps to increase the trust in the ideal of perfection. This perspective reflects the secret identity and the perceived identity biases that are part of the root cause. The same part of our mind that is doing the research is simply confirming the root causes.

The guy is searching for a solution, and in this model of indignity, the solution seems like he will become the "perceived identity." If he can become the positive, strong, caring, and compassionate person he "knows" he is, he can love himself, and the woman will love him, and all will be all right. He can't see that the imagined picture is created in his mind.

THERE ARE OTHER ISSUES WITH THIS STRATEGY

A man's conviction that he is a perceived identity is compromised by his perception that he is not "good enough." Secret identity values generate a sense of indignity. Looking great will mitigate at times, but the sense of indignity must go on before the perceived identity is dealt with.

Also, when the guy pulls off being the ideal perceived identity, the secret identity values will make a part of him feeling like a fake. According to secret identity, he's not exactly "great" and he's not "worthy." He's going to feel untrue regardless of such contradictory values. The sensation of being a cheat also arises as people applaud his achievements. The more success and praise he gets that suits the perceived identity, the more pronounced the secret identity raises suspicions in his head. He cannot be of moral honesty as long as he connects his personality with one or more contradictory images of his head.

The man's ability to control his reaction must keep him on guard against an eruption of resentment and rage. That "on watch" feeling is born out of fear that at some moment it can fall, and guilt will consume his mind. Not only does this sense of fear affect a person, but it suppresses desire and does not make it possible to experience true love and joy.

Creating strong positive values and a healthy self-image will help to reduce the response side but to a small degree. It's a fix that can support others, but still, to base credibility on a fake impression and not on honesty and dignity. This does little to resolve the feelings that emerge from the secret identity s or the convictions of indignity that are at the root of the actions. We are always buried in the subconscious and resurface later in moments of tension when they become more harmful, when we are least able to cope with them.

EMOTION AND FALSE ASSUMPTIONS INFLUENCE ACTIONS

When you look at the action of envy and anger as a way of manipulating and holding others in line, behavior doesn't make sense. Rage and envy are not going to be dear to anyone who is closer to us. The guy in the scenario will also look at his own actions and find that it doesn't make any sense. As a result of his actions, he will see the woman withdraw from him. Yet seeing the outcome and understanding it scientifically does not alter the nature of his actions. Why?

His behavior is not motivated by thought, reasoning, or logical understanding. Therefore, these modalities cannot be modified. It's motivated by biases, distorted images, perspectives, and feelings. When we want to improve our actions, we will approach these basic elements in a way that is separate from mere reasoning and logic. Why do you choose an approach that is distinct from rationality and logic? The inner judge would use reasoning and logic to make decisions and confirm current false convictions.

GETTING RESULTS

Changing attitudes, negative responses, and destructive behavior is about changing your point of view, paying attention, and dissolving false assumptions in your head. Once you learn to change your point of view, you can actually transfer your self out of confidence and out of emotion. From a different point of view, you will be conscious of the flawed reasoning behind the actions of the conviction. Conscious of the false assumptions behind your actions, you should be able to withdraw from harmful acts. Eliminating false assumptions will remove the causes of the feelings. It is the removal of false perceptions that dissolves fear.

When you have the motivation to improve your jealous and angry behavior, you will ultimately have to do more than research the issue. You're going to have to take action.

FORMS TO FIGHT THE JEALOUSY IN RELATIONSHIPS

1. Be respectful of one another's feelings.

When you can admit that jealousy is inevitable, it's almost as important as your spouse. The last thing you need is someone lashing out at you the moment you remind them to give you a short text if they stay out late. "You surrender your independence while you're in a serious relationship," "You have a responsibility for how the other person feels." Some of the worst ways to deal with a jealous partner suggest, "It's your fault!" and, "I said, "I have done nothing!" What helps is warmth, and if you think about frustration as a way to weep out, the solution to that can be affirmation, saying, "I understand where you're coming from." You have to be open and listen and ways you can help your partner feel more at ease, and then consider if their needs are possible. Also, in exchange, you would deserve nothing less.

2. Know that jealousy (in small doses) is a positive indication.

Jealousy doesn't happen without a cause. It's always more than your partner enjoys their ex bikini pic. "You don't have that much money or that much to lose when you start dating anyone," Leahy says. "As the relationship progresses and you are more linked, you become more likely to experience envy in the relationship. The partner is angry because this relationship matters. "Whether you're committed to this guy at all, you're going to have an explosion of jealousy, no matter how cold or logical you want to be. Yet that's a positive thing because it means you care for the working relationship. Recognizing and understanding that this is natural and going on is much much better than beating yourself up or believing it never happens.

3. Set aside time for jealousy.

When you have intense jealous about your partner's sexy coworker or ex-girlfriend (and you know that 1,000 percent of you have nothing to think about), there are activities you can use to cope with.

"'Jealousy Time' is the appointment that the individual makes for their jealous feelings," Leahy says. "When you have a jealous idea at 10 a.m., you write it down and then set it back before the moment of envy." Basically, you take 20 very self-conscious minutes encouraging yourself to thoroughly focus on your emotions, and then you move on. "By the time you get to the point of envy, you're either no longer that interested, or it's the same feeling you've had countless times," he says.

Or if you want to go a little further, you can try what Leahy called the "boredom technique"—repeating a scenario like "my wife could cheat on me" over or over for 10 minutes before you're practically done of it. (Once again, this only happens if you are sure that your partner is trustworthy and that there is no real reason for your feelings).

4. Reduce the standards.

When you believe it's unfair for your wife never to be drawn to someone else, you may need to test your core values, Leahy says. It's totally normal to find other people appealing, but it's not appropriate to rely on that desire or do anything about it. "The laws that people can have will make them more vulnerable to envy," Leahy says. When you have extremely romanticized expectations about your spouse, you're apt to get jealous, like, a lot.

5. Reassess toxic practices.

The very acts you think are going to comfort you (such as interrogating their friend, searching their emails, tracking their ex on social media) will make you more nervous if you don't really discover anything. "These coping mechanisms motivate the same person you're trying to relate to," Leahy says. Even while he acknowledges that, yeah, sometimes your wife is a cheater, and you'd never know more about cheating but staring at their Facebook posts, you also have to make sure the tracking doesn't become an ingrained routine that eventually takes over your life.

6. Know the cheating is not going to kill you.

"Research suggests that people who feel that they would have no substitute if the relationship is ended are far more likely to be jealous," says Leahy. Codependency makes a relationship one that cannot fail in your opinion, and you become more likely to ruminate and become paranoid over any potential risks.

Jealousy will make you understand how important a partner is to you or make you pick up hidden red flags. All it can't do is discourage your friend from sending flirty DMs or cheating on you with a coworker. Everything you can do is express your feelings better to make sure your anger doesn't overwhelm you. You can't manage anything else, but you can surely live.

Chapter 4

HOW TO LOVE YOURSELF

Sometimes it appears to be simpler to adore others than to cherish yourself, however, self-acknowledgment is an essential piece of building solid associations with others. Luckily, with a little arrangement and development, you can likewise figure out how to cherish yourself.

BUILD UP YOUR INNER VOICE

Resolve negative convictions about yourself. The vast majority experience difficulty relinquishing the negative considerations they have about themselves. Such adverse considerations additionally originate from outside individuals whose conclusions we regard and from whom we look for affection and acknowledgment.

Avoid hairsplitting. Numerous individuals experience issues remembering anything short of perfection from themselves. In the event that you end up looking for compulsiveness and getting awful about yourself when you're not exactly perfect, make three straightforward strides. Stop the present line of reasoning. At that point, focus on the responsibility expected to progress in the direction of a target, and afterward include the exertion required.

Moving your consideration from the last item (which can be decided regarding "flawlessness") to the dedication behind a vocation (which is increasingly hard to measure as "great") will assist you with valuing your own great work.

Dispose of the negative channel. Focusing on life-long issues is a negative pattern of behavior. Unreasonable emphasis on horrifying or less tempting lifelong occasions that make such occasions too critical. When you end up believing that everything that transpires is terrible, try to find a little proof despite what you might expect; it is extremely rare that it is truly terrible. Always call yourself names. Calling yourself a name transforms you from a person to a single element of yourself that you don't like.

Saying "I'm such a loser" after being fired from a career is wrong and unfair to you. Instead, make a helpful statement, "I lost my job, but I can use this vision to find and keep a new job." To think that "I am too stupid" is also plausible and reductive." Don't believe the worst will happen. It can be easy to assume that each scenario produces the worst result. However, adjusting your inner thoughts rationally or honestly will help you avoid the generalization or misunderstanding that results from the worst.

- Now edit your internal file.

- Consider the list very unique.

- Give yourself the luxury of your life.

- Celebrate and praise yourself for it.

Build a strategy to deal with failures or disappointments. Consider what threatens you to move away from your new course of self-love and decide whether to deal with such things. You understand that you cannot influence the words and deeds of others, however, you can regulate your emotions and responses.

You may find that the adverse observations of a specific individual, such as your mother or boss, are putting you in a spiral of pessimism. When this happens consistently, try to understand that it is so. Conclude how you will manage the negative emotions you have. You may need to be given the opportunity to meditate or relax. Perceive your feelings and transform your negative reactions into a productive fortification of your trust.

Visit your psychiatrist. Investigating negative considerations and discovering the purposes behind your feelings can arouse emotions or encounters from your past that are difficult to manage.

A therapist who has experience dealing with the traumatic past will help you get through the healing process without allowing you to relive difficult memories.

A therapist's office can be a great place to learn how to treat your negative thoughts productively and recognize your positive qualities.

MAKE POSITIVE STATEMENTS EVERY DAY

Identify those positive considerations that will help you feel more grounded and review them consistently.

A decent positive statement to cultivate self-esteem is: "I am a whole, commendable individual, and I respect, trust and love myself." If you find that validations don't help isolate, try visiting a consultant and looking for an astonishing treatment that also joins various systems.

Get involved in things that make you happy and feel excited. Take what it takes to feel positive in various ways; it may include yoga, reflection, dance and maintaining a positivity diary. Find a program that makes you feel comfortable and respect it.

Do not hesitate to take advantage of the time alone and enjoy it!

Reflect on the results of self-love. When you spend time having fun and supporting yourself, you are sure to find results in other aspects of your life. Note if you have more time or if you can be more collaborative with others. You may begin to feel that you are more responsible for the choices you make and have more control over your life.

PRACTICE MEDITATION

Identify adverse reactions to positive statements that you have. If you have pessimistic thoughts when hearing these affirmations, avoid what causes those negative thoughts. Identify people you have difficulty expressing true love for. Repeat your comments and talk about these people.

Dream of someone you're feeling good about. Repeat the statements and keep the person in mind while you repeat them.

Talk of someone you are not indifferent of. Repeat the affirmations, bearing in mind the person you feel indifferent about.

Enable the affirmations to fill you absolutely with positivity. Repeat the affirmations without actually speaking about anyone. Rather emphasize on the positivity of the claims. Enable the positivity feelings to fill you totally and take the positivity out to the entire world from yourself.

Repeat one more love chant. When you've expanded positivity thoughts everywhere, utter the following mantra: "Let all living human beings experience and be good, and safe." Utter this phrase five times as you hear the words echo in your body and reach out to everyone throughout the world.

UNDERSTAND SELF-LOVE

Realizing the risks of an absence of self-esteem. Lack of self-esteem can lead you to make dangerous decisions. The absence of self-esteem also equates to an absence of self-respect which adds to conscious or unaware self-harm and prevents individuals from taking care of their main needs.

The absence of self-esteem may require negative certification for others. According to others, persistence also allows people to put aside their desires in order to collect the help of others.

The absence of self-esteem can also frustrate mental recovery and progress; an investigation found that individuals who enjoy self-love and ignore each other have more unpleasant results.

See the estimate of early experiences in creating some great memories. Father-son affiliations have long-lasting ramifications for character progression; children who have not met physical, social and lead needs may have long-lasting problems with little certainty.

The antagonistic messages reached the young people – in particular the monotonous messages – regularly bind to the individual's brain and influence their acknowledgments later along the way.

For example, a young man who is informed that he is "boring" or "grueling" will likely imagine he is boring or grueling as an adult, regardless of whether there is evidence despite what one might expect, (for example, having a lot of companions, make people laugh or have a fascinating way of life).

See how guardians should cultivate trust. Guardians should follow the accompanying advice to help their young people's confidence: tune in to their children; expanding their trust.

It may very well be quick to "freeze" a child who gets busy, who generally does not tune in to what he does. In any case, in case you really listen to him and talk to him/her asking him subsequent questions and noting his comments, he may realize that you consider what he needs are.

Show children in a non-forced way (without punching, screaming or abuse) to improve their safety.

For example, if your child hits another child, you should bring him to the side and gently remind him that he should not touch other children or that he may be injured. If necessary, you can take a short break to relax and regroup before returning to play.

Offer comfort, compassion, support and respect to children without judgment to make them feel worthy of love and acceptance.

If that child of yours reveals that he is irritated by something that seems strange to you (like the setting sun), do not give up his feelings. Recognize his feelings by saying, "I understand why you are disturbed in light of the fact that the sun has set. Then do your best to justify that the situation cannot be reversed by saying something like," The sun has to go down every night because the world turns and people on the other side of the planet need the sun. It also gives us the opportunity to relax and prepare for the next day. "In the end, extend a hug or other physical affection and console the child to let him know that you are empathizing with him/her even if you cannot change the situation. Understand the effects of external feedback on love for yourself. You will experience disappointment in your self-love cannot be made in a vacuum without the inside.

Chapter 5

UNDERSTANDING FEAR OF ABANDONMENT

Fear of abandonment is a complex phenomenon in psychology that is believed to originate from childhood deprivation or trauma. This fear has been researched from a variety of perspectives.

The hypotheses underlying fear of loss include interruptions in the natural growth of young children's social and emotional capacities, previous interactions and personal experiences, and susceptibility to common expectations and concepts.

While it is not an official phobia, fear of abandonment is one of the most prevalent and most destructive fears of all. Persons with fear of abandonment that continue to exhibit compulsive habits and patterns of thought that influence their relationships, potentially leading to the alienation they fear becoming a reality.

This uncertainty could be crippling. Knowing this anxiety is the first step in overcoming it.

WHY THAT HAPPENS

Our attitudes and acts in modern relationships are all assumed to be the product of old experiences and acquired lessons that have taken place in adolescence. There are several hypotheses that seek to explain the fear of abandonment.

OBJECT CONSTANCY

In the philosophy of item relations, an offshoot of Freudian thought, an "object" in one's mind is either an individual, a part of an individual, or something that somehow symbolizes one or the other. Object constancy is the idea that even though we can't see others, the entity doesn't shift profoundly.

It is linked to the theory of "object permanence" first explored by the social psychologist Jean Piaget. Children know that mommy or daddy goes to work and then returns home. He or she doesn't stop loving the kid only because they're apart for a couple of hours. In the meantime, the infant creates an abstract entity or a symbolic image of the parent that meets the child's desire for touch during the intervening period.

Item constancy usually occurs before the age of three. As children grow up and mature, separation times become prolonged and sometimes produced by the child when he, say, goes to school or spends the weekend at a friend's home. A kid with a strong object constancy knows that essential relationships are not impaired over time.

The constancy of the entity can be disrupted by stressful events. Death or divorce are common factors, but even circumstances that seem fairly unimportant to the adults concerned can influence the creation of this vital understanding.

For example, children with military parents, those whose parents have no time to spend with them, and those with ignored parents may often be at risk of disturbing object constancy.

ARCHETYPES AND MYTHOLOGY

Mythology is packed with tales of lost or discarded loves, mainly women who devote themselves to their husbands only to be left behind when the lover goes to conquer the world.

Several researchers, including Carl Jung, claim that these beliefs and traditions have become part of our cultural unconscious. On a primary point, we have internalized those archetypes and myths and made them part of our common worldview.

We each have a particular myth — one that isn't shared with others but exists deep inside the heart of our selves. This particular narrative is made up of our experiences of the collective unconscious through the lenses of our own experience.

In this view, fear of loss is similar to these common beliefs, but it ranges in magnitude due to our own personal memories.

PAST EXPERIENCES

There are many concerns caused by the events of our history. However, if the object's constancy is preserved and you are not influenced by universal theories or archetypes, you might have been discarded at some stage throughout the existence. One research showed that our brains ripple right before we remember an occurrence that can be focused on a sound, a scent, or a sensation.

By the time we became teenagers, most of us have experienced some major changes — the loss of a loved one, the leaving of a relative, the dissolution of a relationship, the transition from high school to college to marriage and parenthood. Although most of us adapt to changing conditions, it's not uncommon to be caught somewhere in the process of mourning for what was once.

When you have gone through abrupt and painful loss, such as losing someone through abuse or disaster, you might be at an elevated risk of experiencing this anxiety.

TYPES OF FEAR OF ABANDONMENT

This can be less evident than overt alienation, but it is no less painful. We've all got mental needs. Unless you don't fulfill those needs, you can feel unrecognized, unloved, and disconnected. You can feel really sad, particularly though you're in a relationship with someone who's physically there.

If you have suffered an emotional loss in the past, particularly as a child, you can live in constant fear that it will happen again.

FEAR OF ALIENATION IN CHILDHOOD

It's completely common for babies and toddlers to go through a period of separation anxiety.

We can scream, shout, or refuse to let go when a parent or primary caregiver needs to leave. Children at this point have a hard time knowing whether or where the person is coming back.

When they begin to realize the loved ones aren't coming back, their fears intensify. In most babies, this happens on their third birthday.

ABANDONMENT FEAR IN RELATIONSHIPS

You might be afraid to let yourself be insecure in a relationship. You may have problems with confidence and think so much about the relationship, which could make you wary of your friend.

Over time, the anxieties can lead the other person to step back, perpetuating the loop.

SIGNS OF ANXIETY OF ABANDONMENT

Thousands of people are coping with anxiety. In reality, almost 10% of people have some kind of phobia. Once it comes to partnerships, the underlying habits include:

- You are eager to connect, often to unwanted spouses or partnerships.

- You are hesitant to commit entirely and have had relatively few long-term partnerships.

- You can be able to move on just to make sure you don't get too attached. Please try to do so.

- Among certain women, evidence has also indicated an improvement in the desire to have unprotected sex.

- When in a relationship, you remain, no matter how unhealthy the relationship is.

- You are also impossible to please and nitpicky.

- It is impossible for you to have personal contact.

- You feel insecure and incapable of caring.

- It's hard to believe people.

- It's not a new thing to you to be jealous of anyone you know.

- Feelings of concern over separation are intense.

- Symptoms of general anxiety and depression are normal to you.

- You prefer to overthink everything and try hard to sort out the secret significance of everything.

- You're hypersensitive to criticism.

- You've been repressing resentment and managing things.

- Self-denial is normal to you.

FEAR OF ABANDONMENT: THE EFFECT ON RELATIONSHIPS

Some people are just scared of losing a partner. Many worry that they will unexpectedly find themselves totally isolated. To help understand how individuals with fear of loss can handle a relationship, here is an overview of how a normal relationship can begin and develop. It's especially valid for personal connections, yet there are numerous equals in dear kinships too:

Getting-to-Know-One-Another Phase

At this stage, you have a sense of safety. You're not yet deeply invested in the other guy, so you're only living your life and spending time with your favorite friend.

Honeymoon Period

That is where you want to pledge. You begin investing a ton of energy with the other person, you truly live it up, and you begin to feel great.

Genuine Marriage

The special first nighttime frame can't keep going forever. Regardless of how well two individuals get along, genuine is as yet grinding away. Individuals become ill, have family issues, begin working extended periods of time, consider funds, and need time to complete things.

While this is an extremely common and hopeful stage in a relationship, it might be upsetting for somebody with a fear of dismissal who may consider it to be a sign that the other individual is moving away. In the event that you have this issue, you may be

58

thinking about yourself and making a decent attempt not to share your affections for the issue of being tenacious.

The Slight

Men are individuals. They have flaws and dispositions and stuff on their brains. Regardless of the amount they care for another person, they cannot and ought not generally be compelled to keep that individual at the focal point of their psyches.

Particularly after the special nighttime frame is finished, almost certainly, there will be a minor appearing. That additionally appears as an unanswered instant message, an unreturned call, or a supplication for a couple of days alone.

Response

For the individuals who hazard misfortune, this is a defining moment. At the point when you have that nervousness, you may be totally convinced that the slight is a sign that your better half no longer likes you. What comes next is on the whole directed by the dread of misfortune, its power, and the person's picked adapting strategy.

Numerous individuals battle with this by being tenacious and controlling, demanding that their partner show their love by going through the motions. Some run away, rejecting their partners and being acknowledged. In any case, some accept like the slight is their own and try to transform themselves into a "decent sweetheart" in the endeavor to keep the other individual from leaving.

Truth be told, the slight is presumably not a slight one by any means. Basically, once in a while people simply do things their companions don't appreciate. In a sound relationship, an individual ought to comprehend the circumstance for what it is — an ordinary response that has close to nothing or nothing to do with the relationship. Or then again, he may feel upset about it, however, approach it with either a quiet conversation or a short proclamation. In any case, a solitary situation doesn't turn into a prevailing power on the feelings of the partner.

The Partner's Viewpoint

From the point of view of your partner, the abrupt change in attitude appears to be coming from the wrong direction. In the event that your better half doesn't experience the ill effects of the fear of abandonment, he unquestionably doesn't have even an inkling regarding why his already agreeable, happy spouse is out of the blue being protective and testing, becoming clingy or pulling closer.

Similar to phobias, it's hard to simply speak or justify others out of fear of abandonment. Regardless matter how many times your partner wants to convince you, it's probably not going to be enough. At long last, your conduct propensities and melancholy reactions could alienate your partner, prompting the very suspicion that you fear most.

Adapting techniques

If your tension is moderate and all around controlled, you can have the option to take a few to get back some composure on it effectively by pondering the examples and considering elective social methodologies. For most individuals, though, the fear of abandonment is embedded in deep-seated problems that are impossible to resolve on their own.

Professional help is also required to move past this anxiety to develop the self-confidence needed to actually alter your emotions to behaviors.

Although addressing fear itself is important, it is also necessary to create a sense of belonging. Instead of wasting all your time and attention on a single person, concentrate on creating a community.

Nobody will take care of the entirety of our issues or fulfill the entirety of our needs. In any case, a great network of dear companions will assume a significant job in our lives.

Numerous individuals dread distance since they never feel like they had a "clan" or a "family" when they were growing up. They feel "extraordinary" or detached from others around them for reasons unknown. However, the beneficial thing is, it's rarely past the point of no return.

In the present reality, it's a list of your inclinations, interests, and wishes. Consider others who share their qualities.

Even though unmistakably not every person who communicates an enthusiasm would turn into an old buddy, interests and goals are a fantastic advance in making a strong encouraging group of people. Taking on your inclinations likewise creates fearlessness and the feeling that you're sufficiently solid to manage whatever life tosses your direction.

Mending abandonment issues

If you comprehend the dread of misfortune, there are sure advances you ought to do to keep recuperating.

Hello, yourself to maintain a strategic distance from the pitiless self-judgment. Think of all the positive attributes that make you a good friend and wife.

Speak to the other party about the fear of loss and how it came in. Still be mindful of what you deserve from others. Explain where you're coming from, but don't let them repair your fear of abandonment. Don't expect more than is fair.

Seek to preserve partnerships and develop your social network. Close relationships will improve your self-esteem and sense of belonging.

If this becomes unmanageable, have a go at conversing with an expert advisor. You can profit by one-on-one interaction.

Chapter 6

COPING WITH WORRY

Worries, fears and anxieties are a natural part of your life. It's normal to think about an overdue bill, a pending work interview, or a first date. Yet "natural" concern is overwhelming when it becomes constant and uncontrollable. You consider "what uncertainties" and most pessimistic scenario circumstances consistently, so it meddles with your regular day to day existence.

Constantly stressing, pessimistic thoughts, and constantly assuming the worst will take a toll on your mental and physical wellbeing. This will lessen your enthusiastic vitality, cause you to feel apprehensive and anxious, trigger despair, migraines, stomach agony, and muscle stiffness, and think that it's difficult to concentrate at work or school. They can get the terrible considerations about the individuals closest to them, self-cure with liquor or prescriptions. Incessant uneasiness may likewise be a critical indication of Generalized Anxiety Disorder (GAD), an across the board tension condition that incorporates pressure, apprehension, and a general feeling of disquiet that influences the entire life.

In case you're tormented by over the top dread and worry, there are steps you should take to remove apprehensive contemplations. Constant uneasiness is an apprehensive condition that can be obliterated. You will show the brain how to be quiet and take a look at things from an increasingly serene, less on edge perspective.

WHY IS IT SO HARD TO STOP WORRYING?

Constant stress will take a heavy toll. It will hold you awake at night and make you nervous and edgy in the daytime. In certain psychological worries, nervous feelings are triggered by the belief — both pessimistic and positive — that you are worried about: cynical assumptions about anxiety. You may feel that your excessive attention is dangerous, that it may make you insane or damage your physical health. Perhaps you may fear that you may lose all control of your concern — that it will take over and never stop. Although negative conviction, or worry about worry, adds to your fear and leaves you worrying, optimistic beliefs about concern can be almost as harmful.

Positive feelings regarding the issue. You may feel that your interest helps you escape negative situations, avoids problems, trains you for the worse, or contributes to remedies. You are just persuaded that it is a smart thing to do or the best way to ensure that you don't miss something? It's hard to shake the trap of anxiety because you feel that your interest has a good reason. At the point when you comprehend that the issue is alarming, not the arrangement, you will regain control of your disturbed psyche.

HOW TO STOP WORRYING

BUILD A DAY-TO-DAY "STRESS" CYCLE

It's hard to be successful in your day-to-day tasks when fear and stress overtake your mind and divert you from work, school, or home life. This is the place the strategy of delaying stress will help. As opposed to attempting to delay or dispose of an awkward inclination, authorize yourself to do as such, at that point put off worrying until some other time.

64

Construct a "think cycle." Pick a fixed time and place to think about it. In your time of concern, you're encouraged to think over something on your head. The rest of the day, though, is a space free of anxiety.

Write down some of your questions. If you have an unpleasant thought or concern in your mind throughout the day, make a short note of it and then resume the day. Note that you'll have time to talk about it later, and there's no reason to stress about it right now.

Move down your "anxiety list" at the duration of your anxiety. If the emotions you feel are disturbing you, urge yourself to consider them, yet just for the measure of time you've accommodated your season of concern. When you discuss your issues in this manner, you will also find it easier to gain a more rational viewpoint. So, if your concerns don't seem to matter anymore, just cut your time of concern.

CHALLENGE NERVOUS THOUGHTS

When you have persistent fear and stress, odds are you're looking at the universe in terms that make it feel more daunting than it actually is. For starters, you can overestimate the likelihood that things could turn out poorly, leap to worst-case scenarios automatically, or interpret any nervous thought as though it were a matter of fact. You can even disprove your own ability to deal with life's challenges, believing you break apart at the first hint of difficulty. "If something isn't fine, I'm a complete loser." Overgeneralization from a single bad event is believing it to stay true indefinitely. "I haven't been recruited for the role. "Focusing on the negatives when ignoring the good ones.

Make misleading assumptions without any clear facts. You're behaving like a mind reader: "I can tell you she really hates me." Or a fortune teller: "I just think something bad is going to happen." Accepting that the manner in which you act is a result of the real world. "I have an inclination that I'm such a moron. Somebody will snicker at me. "Keep a clear list of what you can and should not do and punish yourself if you break any of the rules. "I was never going to want to initiate a conversation with her. I'm such a dumb guy." Marking yourself dependent on failures and seeing inadequacies. "I'm a failure; I'm boring; I want to be alone." Taking blame for events outside your influence. "It's my fault that my son was in an accident. I was meant to advise him to drive cautiously in the mud. "How to question these thoughts In your moment of concern, address your pessimistic thinking by reminding yourself: Where is the proof that the hypothesis is true? Isn't that true?

Is there a more optimistic, rational way to look at the situation?

What's the likelihood that what I'm fearful of would really happen? If the likelihood is small, what are some of the more likely outcomes?

Was the thinking helpful? How's it going to help me, and how's it going to hurt me?

What should I say to a friend who was concerned about this?

RECOGNIZING SOLVEABLE AND UNSOLVABLE ISSUES

Evidence recommends that when you are stressed, you are marginally less apprehensive. Playing over the issue in your cerebrum possesses you from your feelings and causes you to have an inclination that you're finishing something. Anyway, there are two very surprising issues to consider to fix issues.

Problem management involves determining the problem, taking practical measures to deal with it, and then bringing the solution into effect. Worrying, on the other hand, never contributes to a solution. Regardless of how much time you waste focusing on worst-case situations, you're able to deal with them should they eventually happen.

Is worry resolvable? Unproductive, unsolvable problems are those on which there is no subsequent intervention. When the fear can be overcome, continue brainstorming. Create a list of all the options you might think of. Try not to be too caught up to find the right answer. Focus on issues that you have the ability to alter, rather than situations or facts beyond your reach. Once you've assessed your choices, make an action plan.

If the fear is not resolvable, embrace the confusion. Unless you're a persistent fighter, the vast majority of your nervous feelings are likely to fall into this camp. Worrying is also the way we try to foresee what the future brings – the way to stop unexpected shocks and monitor the results. The question is that it doesn't work. Focusing in worst-case situations would only deter you from loving the positive stuff you have at present. To stop stressing, discuss the need for clarity and urgent answers.

- Will you like to expect that negative stuff will happen only because they're uncertain?

- Provided that the risk is very remote, it is easy to survive with a slight probability that something bad may happen.

- Tell your friends and family how to cope with confusion in different circumstances.

- Stay in line with the feelings. Worrying over confusion is also a means of suppressing negative feelings.

STOP THE LOOP OF WORRY

If you stress constantly, unpleasant thoughts can appear to run through your mind constantly. You may feel like you're spiraling out of control, going insane, or about to blackout under the weight of all this fear. In any case, there are steps that you should take currently to stop every one of those apprehensive sentiments and give yourself a break from relentless nervousness.

Get up there and get moving. Exercise is a sheltered and fruitful enemy of nervousness treatment that actuates endorphins that mitigate torment and stress, improve essentialness, and fortify your feeling of prosperity. Most explicitly, by simply pondering how your body reacts when you walk, you can stop the steady surge of stresses that experience your brain. Focus on the sound of your feet contacting the ground as you walk, run, or move, for instance, or the pace of your breath, or the impression of sun or wind against your skin.

Taking a yoga exercise or a kendo exercise class. By keeping your thoughts on your movements and breathing, performing yoga or kendo holds your fixation on the occasion, assisting with clearing your musings and add to a quiet perspective.

Ponder that. Contemplation works by changing the consideration from pondering the future or living in the past to what's happening at the present time. You will break the relentless cycle of pessimistic feelings and fears by remaining completely involved in the current moment. Just find a calm, relaxing spot and select one of the many free or affordable mobile applications that can direct you through the meditation process.

Gradual relaxing of muscles. This will assist you with getting away from the steady pattern of tension by focusing your consideration on your body rather than your feelings. By tensioning and afterward loosening up different muscle groups in your body, you soothe muscle aches in your body. So as your body unwinds, your intuitive will comply.

Try to breathe slowly. When you think, you feel nervous and breathe harder, sometimes leading to more fear. Be that as it may, by doing profound breathing activities, you can quiet down your psyche and calm unpleasant musings.

TALKING ABOUT YOUR ISSUES

It can seem like a simple methodology, however talking up close and personal with a dependable companion or relative — somebody who tunes in to you without being addressed, offended or continually sidetracked — is one of the most impressive approaches to loosen up your sensory system and diminish dread. As the issues heighten, pondering them will cause them to appear to be even less risky.

Having you worrying just helps them to pile up until they become intimidating. When the concerns are unjustified, verbalizing them will show what they are — needless worries. So, if your worries are valid, sharing them with someone else will create ideas that you would not have thought about on your own.

Develop a strong support network. We're not supposed to be raised in solitude. But a good support group doesn't automatically mean a large network of friends. Try not to think little of the rewards of a couple of individuals who you can depend and rely on to be there for you. So if you don't believe like you have someone to trust, it's never too late to develop new connections.

Know how to stop when you feel nervous. Your stressful personality can be something you've experienced since you've grown up. If your mother is a persistent addict, she's not the right one to call when you feel anxious — no matter how close you are.

69

EXERCISE MINDFULNESS

Young woman sitting back in a chair that cradles her back, hands crossed in a lap, chin up, eyes closed. Thinking is typically based on the future — what could happen and what you're going to do about it — or on the past, rehashing stuff you've said or done. This technique is focused on noticing your thoughts and then letting them go, allowing you to recognize where your behavior is causing issues and getting in contact with your emotions.

Recognize and consider your questions. Don't want to dismiss, fight, or monitor them as normal. Alternatively, clearly consider them as if from an outsider's point of view, without responding or judging.

Let go of your fears. Note that while you're not struggling to control the nervous feelings that crop up, they'll quickly disappear, like clouds rolling through the sky. It's only because you're immersed in the problems that you get trapped.

Keep concentrated on the present. Pay attention to the way your body sounds, to the pattern of your heartbeat, to the ever-changing feelings, and to the thoughts that float through your head. If you find yourself caught in a single thought, bring your mind back to the present moment.

Rehash each day. Utilizing care to stay concentrated on the moment is a fundamental thought, however, it requires time and practice to appreciate the advantages. You'll likely notice from the start that your psyche props up back to your concerns. If you don't mind, endeavor not to get resentful. Each time you turn your psyche back to the occasion, you build up another psychological schedule that will assist you with breaking free from the terrible circle of concern.

Chapter 7

IMPACTS OF OBSESSED ATTACHMENTS ON COUPLES

If we convinced you that we all know the single biggest indicator of how good a kid is going to do in life and we calculate it, that's amazing, isn't it? Okay, wonder what it is. This is the link.

Attachment is the fundamental mechanism for understanding human relations. That's how much an individual is connected to others. Early interactions create a framework for later life relations. That's why our early interactions, the interactions between a child and her caregivers/parents/adults are so significant. How does it all feel like?

Studies over a variety of years and communities have shown that some 35-40 percent of people say they feel vulnerable in their adult relationships. Although 60-65 percent experience a safe, caring and fulfilling relationship.

How stable or dangerous we are with our intimate partners depends, in part, on how we match up with our parents at a young age. From the day we were born, we looked to our parents (or guardians) for love, comfort and protection, particularly in times of trouble. We call them "attachment statistics" for this purpose.

When our attachment figures respond to our distress in ways that fulfill our needs, we feel comforted and encouraged, our anxiety is minimized, and we know that our attachment figures can be relied on in difficult times.

Yet if parents frequently respond to a child's frustration by relinquishing their feelings, ignoring their requests for assistance, or making the child feel stupid, the child may learn not to trust their attachment figures for support, and to ignore their fears and desires, and to deal with them alone. Such downplaying techniques are referred to as "deactivating attachment techniques."

To some, parents respond to a child's frustration by being incompatible with the care they offer or not offering the same kind of help. Parents might often understand the pain of their infant; often they don't notice the pain or reflect on how the distress made them feel, rather than encouraging the infant to control their emotions.

Certain guardians might be offering care, yet that is not what the youngster needs. Of model, a kid may require inspiration to manage an issue, yet the grown-up is professing to be empathetic and comprehends that the kid will most likely be unable to manage the issue. Day by day presentation to these sorts of child-rearing encounters implies that youngsters will feel extreme uneasiness, especially when overpowered and put forth a lot of attempts to be truly near their connection figures. Such systems of developing significance and finding pointless closeness are designated "hyper activating strategies."

We should investigate the four connection styles and see what they can resemble in grown-ups.

SECURE ATTACHMENT

People with a secured attachment wouldn't fret being relied upon.

They once in a while stress over being abandoned or somebody getting excessively near them. They have positive self-esteem and see others emphatically.

These convictions enable them to request what they need in a relationship or request clearness. They don't feel they need to control or persuade somebody; they are sufficient. This is somebody who doesn't show any sort of desirous or possessive conduct. That is where they don't do everything together, they have their own advantages. They go out with companions just as with one another, they're not envious of one another, they're not possessive, they don't continue checking in with one another, they don't have to keep messaging or calling to see where the other is, on the grounds that they're certain about the relationship. They'll have had a protected connection with their parental figure where they've had a sense of security. It's what Bowlby called "building up a protected base as a youngster." Consider the peek-a-boo game that guardians regularly play. That is somewhat how a youngster begins to discover that somebody can vanish and return. The more that occurs, as long as the parent continues returning, the more secure the kid gets. That empowers the youngster at that point to go to class or go nearby and play with a companion since they trust the parent will be present when they return. What's more, that is the equivalent of seeing someone when they're a grown-up.

This is the thing that we as a whole trust in. On the off chance that a youngster grows up with a safe connection, she comprehends sound connections. She is secure, grounded and expects connections in life that are solid. She can confide in individuals. She can likewise consider and hold others' feelings for them. What this means is a grown-up who can endure troubles in a relationship and use sound adapting aptitudes to deal with these difficulties. Using ethics of anticipating that others should be dependable and strong, individuals with secure connections will in general really cultivate this in their connections. In this way, a kid who experienced childhood in a home with a safe connection will, as anyone might expect, be bound to frame strong, solid grown-up sentimental connections and fellowships, and almost certain and fit for bringing up her own youngsters with a protected connection.

AMBIVALENT INSECURE ATTACHMENT

The on-edge type battles to discover others that need to get as close as they need. They frequently stress that their partner doesn't generally love them or need to remain with them. These convictions will in general, give them a reason to act in manners that strengthen this. They frequently feel that their longing for somebody drives them off.

This sort debases themselves and worships others.

Accordingly, they perform to meet other's desires. They are likewise lacking self-worth, so they look for outer approval for their value, since they don't feel commendable themselves. Studies express that a greater number of ladies than men utilize this procedure. This individual might be bit unreliable in their grown-up connections. They may be on edge, somewhat without self-worth, stressed over [a partner] going out with companions, or them having separate interests. Tragically, what happens is, they cause contentions seeing someone over these things. In extraordinary cases, they could wind up being controlling, possessive and envious. They may begin doing a great deal of checking, even clandestine observation like placing cameras in [a partner's] vehicle. That is the most extraordinary end and oppressive conduct. In case you're in that sort of relationship, it's possibly perilous on the grounds that that individual has no resistance at all of you being not their absolute belonging. Somebody who's not had a very safe connection [to their caregiver]. Where the guardians weren't in every case there when required and they won't have constantly paid their youngster as much attention as they required.

If you will review, this connection style is increasingly normal in kids whose guardians were conflicting – now and then present (both sincerely and truly), and here and then not. These kids regularly present as profoundly restless. As grown-ups, youngsters who grew up with this style of connection might be excessively sensitive to their partner. Believing others is troublesome and thusly, they may become hyper-mindful of the other individual and excessively centered around little subtleties. For instance, they may consider what the other individual is thinking, or why he hasn't called throughout the day, or where he is at a specific second. It very well may be more enthusiastically for somebody who was raised with this connection style to trust and accept that friends and family will finish or stick around. As you can envision, this kind of conduct can push others away. For grown-ups with an irresolute connection style, this pulling endlessly is regularly met with endeavors to pull friends and family back. The challenges emerge when similar practices that really pushed one away (e.g., questions, uncertainties, addressing) are similar practices used to pull others back in. Two individuals who share this connection style in a relationship are regularly riotous together – fluctuating among close and far off, battling to confide in one another, and accepting the other should "simply know" what different needs without inquiring.

AVOIDANT-INSECURE

This "disregard me" type is awkward with close enthusiastic connections. At the point when this sort was more youthful, it's imaginable their folks were inaccessible. Therefore, this sort doesn't prefer to rely upon others or have others rely upon them. They have to feel free and independent since they discovered that closeness causes more agony than disconnection.

Their autonomy is strengthened into their excessively positive self-perspectives and negative view of others. They will in general utilize the frailty of anxious type to approve their autonomy.

Their dread of duty with an anxious fortifies their haughtiness. This sort will, in general, end up in an unfulfilling relationship in the wake of an unfulfilling relationship.

As per a similar research, 70% of the populace holds similar convictions and desires in adulthood that they framed in their adolescence. This is the reason our initial connections sway our grown-up connections in such huge manners. Every connection procedure is pulled into different techniques in truly unsurprising ways. A few people who might fit into this style simply don't make connections. They maintain a strategic distance from them altogether and discover it unfathomably hard to identify with others since they can't trust by any stretch of the imagination. Or, then again, they attempt and make connections; however, they think that its troublesome and the relationship just keeps going a long time. They may begin being unbelievably depressed and that puts the other individual off, and it just finishes. It's that satisfying the happiness since they don't anticipate that the relationship should work, and lo and see, it doesn't. They keep re-persuading themselves regarding their conviction that they're not deserving of a relationship. They may likewise show self-disrupting practices. Kids who'd been in treatment for quite a while would be hesitant to reconnect with their folks once they were permitted to see them. "He saw phases of dissent, and that if a kid is isolated from a parent it will cry and cry," Barbara says. "In the long run it will surrender. Maybe the youngster has settled on a choice that says, 'you're not going to be there for me, I'm going to abandon you and be autonomous.'" If that occurs, that is the most dire outcome imaginable. The child limits absolutely from the parent or gatekeeper. You in like manner watch this infrequently with an adolescent whose parent has an impulse. The child twists up not solely being self-ruling, yet moreover dealing with the watchmen similarly as themselves at an especially young age.

This connection style will in general outcome when a kid has guardians who were reliably not present or were cavalier. Thus, these kids start to encounter the world as a spot where others can't be depended upon and frequently have neglected enthusiastic needs. As grown-ups, this can show as dread of closeness or intimacy. These people are regularly reluctant to get excessively near others inspired by a paranoid fear of being harmed – naturally, they feel an inborn need to secure themselves. Also, if your youth encounters instruct you to concentrate on and deal with yourself, it tends to be hard as a grown-up to be receptive to other people and instinctually notice when others need support. This can appear to others as childish or unapproachable when in all actuality, it might be a dread of the weakness that accompanies setting one's own needs aside to help another person. Defenselessness is hard for everybody, except all the more so for individuals whose powerlessness has verifiably been met with dissatisfaction or harmed. In sentimental connections, individuals with this connection style may pull away from an partner during times of trouble or may battle to draw near by any stretch of the imagination. Furthermore, as guardians, they may make some hard memories understood and associating with their kids in an adjusted and close manner.

DISORGANIZED-INSECURE

As we learn from the study of attachment, disorganized-insecure is the most negative of attachment types. It appears to happen because parents become inconsistent; from loving attitudes to others that are scary or terrifying. Sadly, adolescents who grow up in this kind of setting often struggle with life-long relationships. Their partnership can be defined by a willingness to be close while at the same time keeping others apart. Within the most serious situations, relationships between adults with this type of attachment can include physical or psychological abuse. Adults who have grown up in such a disorganized household often fail to recognize their own abilities to self-regulate, and often pursue someone to satisfy the void. Within a disorganized attachment environment, children do not know what safe, rational discipline and caring looks like. As a result, they are often unable to provide their own children with this sort of partnership when they are parents. A person who was born in a disorganized family environment might not realize why a child needs it, and might not have the sense of what it is like to be nurtured, or how to give it to others.

However, the challenge that arises when we have such definitions is that few of us fall into just one. Most of us have complicated backgrounds, and we find that we take pieces of both, and contribute to one, but have characteristics that are often associated with others. I want to make sure that all sorts of generalizations are not meant to categorize or diagnose individuals. So, I'm not thinking about it to excuse or condone negative conduct. So why do you share this? Okay, I strongly agree that there is no potential to improve without knowledge. Once we begin to understand why we or our loved ones are doing these things, we will be constructive and do something about it. It may mean doing some of the same things and helping our children develop the same good skills as we have. In some, it can involve self-reflection about our heritage as well as our present relationships. They also learn that we have a parent's way of being parented, and to some degree, that's real. Yet – it's a major, important thing – we don't have to. At the point when we increase and build up our mindfulness, we upgrade and fortify our ability to be increasingly proactive in our associations and how we coach our youngsters.

When we respond emotionally to something, we should ask ourselves, "Am I responding to what's going on in this moment, or am I unconsciously falling into the routines of my past?" If we are stressed out, we are more likely to return to a less structured parenting style, particularly if our norm is focused on an unhealthy attachment style.

We love relationships that reflect our insecurity: if you pay careful attention to the intimate relationships of your friends and family, you'll find very simple trends.

You'll find that security stays in love with security, even though these insecurities come up differently.

Broad interactions elicit similar reactions. Such reactions are then made an interpretation of so as to avow our verifiable presumptions about ourselves as well as other people. Hitched couples with poor connection would disregard their life partner who sees them distinctively before they are seen by their life partners in the way they see themselves. Especially in dating, individuals with skeptical self-sees frequently look for life partners who give troublesome decisions to approve their self-see. So, what's making this so hard? Such experiences are much easier at the outset of the relationship, as their pathologies help their self-confidence. People with pessimistic (anxiety) self-views are more associated with partners who judge them favorably (avoidant) given the fact that they are unlikely to be able to change themselves.

WILL THEY CHANGE OVER TIME?

Our connection styles are viewed as generally stable all through life, however, a few people will in general move from a flimsy connection to a more secure connection type. Be that as it may, it doesn't simply occur, it takes a ton of work.

Research shows that while attachment patterns can become more difficult to alter as we mature, life events and interactions that contradict our pre-existing views about relationships may contribute to improvements in our attachment style.

Marriage and the formation of common interests that affirm affection and loyalty to others have been reported to alleviate relationship anxiety. But incidents that are perceived as a threat to one's relationship or a lack of contact (such as partner rejection) can increase attachment vulnerability.

HOW ARE YOU GOING TO BOOST YOUR SECURITY?

Growing someone's sense of safety can be achieved in a number of ways. One includes access to words or pictures that foster feelings of affection, warmth and attachment (such as showing viewers a video of a mother carrying an infant, a couple hugging an infant, or phrases such as "hug" and "kiss"). Another is to make them recall past events when they were comforted by a human.

Another tactic has explored whether couples can help assist each other to reduce or mitigate relationship anxiety. Preliminary evidence shows that helping people feel comfortable and improving their self-confidence is a positive approach for someone with a high degree of attachment anxiety.

That could be the safest option for people who are high in attachment avoidance not to be as aggressive and hostile during a confrontation or when coping with interpersonal problems.

In the area of relationship therapy, a psychological technique called Emotionally Focused Relationships Therapy (EFCT) has been introduced to tackle the negative effects of attachment distress in married couples and has been shown to be successful.

EFCT works on breaking loops of unpleasant experiences between couples, and on helping both to cope with each other's relationship issues and worries, such as rejection and abandonment. Couples then learn from the therapist how to express more efficiently each other's relationship needs for affection, warmth and support.

The search for a stable and caring interpersonal bond is a huge struggle for everyone, but successful potential partnership interactions have the ability to transfer people from a place of uncertainty to a place where intimacy, approval and warmth can be found.

ROLE OF COUNSELING IN INSECURE RELATIONSHIP

Defining your relationship type as insecure or avoidable is not always a bad thing, and it certainly doesn't mean that you can never have a healthy relationship. If people have therapy or treatment, they can get a lot of help until they begin to understand why they have specific problems in building relationships. When people can make a correlation with their childhood experience, they can begin to try to behave differently.

While counselors can support people who fit in any form, the more severe the behavior (especially with extreme detachment) is. We may say that their brain is almost hard-wired into their current behavior, and it's very hard to get them out of it. Cognitive-behavioral approaches can function quite well for people, especially in the area of anxiety. If someone is at home and their partner is out and they want to keep calling or messaging them to figure out where they are, it'll show them the strategies to deal with it. It will even look at how they're feeling and catastrophizing. It could be really good.

WELL-INTENTIONED ACTIONS THAT CAN HARM A RELATIONSHIP

Being a good spouse is not always straightforward, and most people really want to do their best as a spouse.

There are, however, certain things that the partners are trying to do to be supportive, which can only make matters harder. Review this list to see if you're going to slip into any of these bad habits.

PROVIDING ADVICE

If your partner comes to you with a problem, it's always too easy to find out how to fix it, isn't it? It's false. Offering advice also sends a message that you don't really know or that you don't care about it. It's a lot easier to listen and be a "sounding board" or a "shoulder to cry on" than to propose remedies.

Once you have a reasonable idea of the issue, you will be able to make any recommendations, but not until you have a direct question or an explanation that your advice is needed.

Being the "Devil's Advocate" falls in the same grouping. Like a decent friend, you want to be by your partner's side rather than let them see what's wrong with their point. If they don't ask you to support their excuses, don't offer to. Your relationship is the most important thing to remember. Have confidence in your decision of a partner. You married a smart guy, and he or she would finally work it out. They just need someone on their side.

BEING TOO POSITIVE

In any relationship, positivity is necessary. Living at the positives and what's privilege is such a great amount of simpler than concentrating on the awful and what's "out." Nevertheless, it's not really good to try to move your partner into a bad situation by promoting "looking for the bright side" or thinking about disturbing issues. Perhaps you've got to live with sad, upset, irritated, or angry thoughts.

When you try to change your attitude, you risk the likelihood that your partner will believe that his or her desires and interests have been overlooked. You may also be at risk of witnessing vulnerability and learning about your partner and your relationship. Listen to your companion before you attempt to change your attitude or speech. Ask a lot of questions to get him or her to talk more about something that worries you.

PROTECTING BY NOT REVEALING GRIEVANCES OR RELEVANT INFORMATION

The tendency may be to disregard issues rather than deal with them. What someone doesn't know, after all, can't hurt them, right? Secrets may be very damaging to a family. Hiding items from bills and budgets will destroy the confidence and reputation of a partnership.

Not being transparent about important issues that concern you will lead to tension in a relationship, too. Maintaining stability does not necessarily translate to a better relationship.

HOLDING YOUR PARTNER'S DESIRES HIGHER THAN YOUR OWN AND NOT TAKING PROPER CARE OF YOURSELF

There are a lot of people...including men...in marriages that dedicate a lot of time to having their spouse and their families satisfied. While that seems like it's the best thing to do most of the time, there's a high chance of burnout.

Many who do a lot in a relationship very frequently find that their standards of reciprocation are not fulfilled, which leads to pain and frustration.

You know what the air hostess state, isn't that right? Put on your own breathing mask before you put it on somebody else. The equivalent is valid in relationships. Assume responsibility for your own physical and passionate wellbeing and you will be a lot more joyful partner.

Chapter 8

RELATIONSHIP AND THE ROLE OF MUTUAL BLAME

These are just a couple of instances of how individuals accuse each other. I'm certain you will think of more progressively about your own connections. What is important to remember about collective remorse is that it rarely works. It is typically in the form of disputes where a couple starts to indulge in a cycle of reciprocal responsibility. When this happens, a person begins to be more aggressive and angrier than at the beginning. This is letting you know you are at fault for something that says you are inept, to a fault, and to be frail in different regards. No man needs to be back in the corner and compelled to admit that he's wrong. When one's pride and reputation are concerned, it is important to prove the other person wrong, and then accuse him. In reality, despite realizing that they are to blame for something, the person would argue that they are to blame. For example, a man was presumably asked to buy a bottle of milk. Nonetheless, since they were in the midst of the fight, he undoubtedly denied that he had misunderstood and blamed her.

The substance of the relationship is to such an extent that everybody is to blame and, somehow or another, everybody prompts the issue. In other words, people in a relationship have an effect in hundreds of ways. Truth be told, it's far-fetched that anybody is completely to fault for a large number of the things that occur. Relating implies that there are associations between two individuals who share a past and a future together. Association doesn't imply that one partner prompted the other to occur. Every person is responsible for his or her own actions, independent and distinct from the other. Another example may be that "I stopped engaging because of your criticism" actually means "I feel like I want to stop when I hear the criticism." An old example is that "you gave me a headache." Why blame that on someone else?

At the end of the day, in a dispute, it is easier to consider solutions to settle the argument. Perhaps it's as easy as having a different way to phrase things. Communication is more than one individual talking. Or maybe, communication includes listening first, and afterward reacting in a non-protective way. For example, the use of the pronoun "I" while speaking is much preferable than the accusatory "You." Often, the use of the word "Why" as "Why Do You" is accusatory. It sounds a lot nicer to say, "I'm so upset that I was laid off that I want to blame everybody." Another way is to say, "I wish we could find a compromise that you'd consider reasonable." Choosing words is often necessary.

In a lifelong partnership, the goal would not be to win a point at the detriment of the other person, especially if you love the person. In tight connections, winning a contention can mean losing a companionship.

Seek answers rather than a fault.

KEY RELATIONSHIP PROBLEMS YOU MUST PREVENT

It is of course of the utmost importance to work on areas that can develop, construct and push your partnership to the next level. Around the same time, though, we must be mindful of the errors committed by other partners to undermine and ruin their marriages in irreparable ways.

The following are some things that you can remember and be cautious about in case you're attempting to make a solid, sound enduring and productive relationship:

AVOID PICKING ON PARTNER'S FAULTS

No one gets a kick out of the chance to be judged, especially the one they love, so abstain from singling out your partner's shortcomings. You're not faultless yourself, so don't anticipate that your partner should be perfect either. Respect them for what they are, value them for their imperfection, and regard them for the certified greatness that falsehoods covered up underneath the outward appearance.

AVOID COMPLACENCY

Most marriages collapse simply because the pair is getting so complacent and relaxed inside the relationship. As human beings, we are hungry for novelty and diversity in our lives. At first, toward the start of the relationship, we experience a few new feelings and furthermore partake in occasions that produce anticipation, disarray and unusualness.

At the point when you've been dating somebody for some time, it's anything but difficult to totally overlook the reasons that initially produced the flash and energy in your relationship. At the point when you find that you are being messy and that your relationship is getting so exhausting, realize that at some point or another, one of you should plan something to spice it up, or, more than likely, the relationship is going to self-destruct, both intellectually and literally.

STOP INSTANT GRATIFICATION

It's exceptionally simple to get dependent on causing your partner to fulfill all the inward wishes and wants. Remember that despite the fact that you're seeing someone, still be a different individual with one beating heart and one brain. Dependence on your partner can well add to destitution, which can cause your partner to feel claustrophobic in your quality. Or maybe, consider being content with yourself when your partner isn't there. Additionally, work on satisfying your psychological, physical, good and material needs in a positive way, without requiring your partner to be there constantly.

At long last, understand that any relationship requires love and closeness the same amount as it requires a little partition and space. Thus, be mindful so as not to be snared.

STOP CARRYING OLD BAGGAGES

By old baggage, I'm not talking about old bags that have been sitting in that wardrobe for quite a long time. Rather, I mean individuals, emotions, and discernments that trap you before and debilitate you from going on with your new relationship right now. Stay consistent with yourself by relinquishing the past and by thinking about your relationship with everything that is in you now.

MAINTAIN A STRATEGIC DISTANCE FROM UNREASONABLE ASSUMPTIONS

Get over in your mind that your partner can fix your relational troubles or confidence issues. Your partner is human; they can help you, yet you don't depend on them to help you with any inquiry that compromises you consistently. It's very intellectually debilitating and you will consume your partner's psychological vitality. You need to recall that they're, despite everything, battling with their very own issues at home, busy working, and wherever else they're experiencing life. Better believe it, love one another, and be there when your partner needs you most, however, don't cling to the bogus expectations that this relationship will offer you genuine satisfaction at any phase of your life.

Connections are not supernatural occurrence medicates that you can fly at any second, yet rather cherishing lifesavers that can help make your life change both less complex and progressively charming.

QUIT CONSTRAINING YOUR PARTNER TO MODIFY

It plays on the thought of accomplishment once more. You're not great, so don't anticipate that your companion should be immaculate either. Think back to your initial want and how you felt about your partner at that point. Do you criticize about any single thing you don't care for about them, or do you just appreciate them in light of what their identity resembled, an aggregate and magnificent heap of imperfections and everything? Your relationship has met up and you clearly praised each other's abilities and shortcomings. Prop this network up by attempting to be viable where it is powerless or proficient where it may be insufficient. Let yourself know, does the world truly need me to have another clone?

Value your partner for what their identity is and endeavor to try to accomplish the quality/shortcoming balance that is obvious in every single positive organization.

Until you can't help contradicting your companion, despite the fact that I show that my perspective is correct, is it worth causing my partner to feel awful about the way that they're off-base?

Let's all grow up and stop behaving like little girls. What is right and what is wrong is meaningless, as long as what is most important remains unchanged until it is finished and done.

ABSTAIN FROM CREATING NEGATIVE ANCHOR

This is the typical outcropping of the previously mentioned point. At whatever point we experience a solid and agonizing enthusiastic expression, all inside our present world is clearly associated with the passionate condition. It implies that in the event that you get back home from work feeling upset and pass that fury to your partner, at that point these sentiments of disappointment will gradually yet step by step keep on implanting themselves in your partner's essence. E.g., the next week you may be coming home from work feeling at the top of the planet, but the moment you see your wife you're beginning to feel insecure and furious, and you just can't understand why? That is proof that tells you that you have a detrimental magnet attached to your partner's body, and it is undoubtedly the biggest and most strong disruptive factor in the relationship of the 21st century. To stop this, really separate yourself from your partner at a second when you are having extraordinary emotions, and attempt to be close to your partner while you are feeling happiness and expectation.

This methodology won't just douse the danger of having negative grapples, it will likewise offer ascent to the likelihood of creating positive relationship building stays.

After going through all these main steps, you will have the requisite techniques to develop and expand on your relationships in amazing ways. Try to be straightforward and reliable. Nothing is ever perfect, and nothing has ever been managed without a little devotion, readiness, and assurance. Keep the cycle fun, entertaining and rewarding, and your partnerships will certainly witness the fruits of your success.

Chapter 9

RELATIONSHIP AND INSECURITY

In a relationship, both partners will feel loved, valued and safe. This holy grail of good relationship features is ripped down where there is significant tension in the relationship.

From envy to behavioral influence, fear can express itself in several detrimental ways. Your marital fear may or may not be rational, but it produces unhealthful conduct irrespective of the rationale.

What is significant is that such vulnerability can also manifest itself in health issues later on, as studies have shown.

Here are eight symptoms of vulnerability in a relationship and what you should do about it.

SIGNS OF INSECURITY

1. Fear of losing someone

One indication that you are vulnerable in a relationship is a persistent fear of losing your partner. Relationship insecurities make you feel like you're not worth anyone's attention, and you find yourself obsessed as to whether your boyfriend really loves you, really enjoys sex, is really drawn to you, finds you irritating, or tries to leave you for anyone else. That concern is all the more understandable after you have gone through a tough time with your partner, where they might have lost your trust.

In reality, a set of studies showed that emotional relationship vulnerability was an indicator of sexual frustration.

Relationship is lost without confidence. If you're still afraid that you're not going to be able to trust your partner, you shouldn't be together. Trust is the cornerstone of a stable partnership.

2. Consuming jealousy

There is a certain degree of envy in a relationship that is considered good. You're in a serious relationship, after all, and you don't want anyone else to ruin what you've set up. Yet there is a phase when this positive envy is turning into a burning fear. Popular signs of jealousy include:

- Cheating on your partner

- Continuously checking your partner's whereabouts

- Aggression

- Manipulating behavior, such as forcing relationships to stop because they make you insecure

- Being too close or sticking to your partner

- Spite and pettiness, such as having a new friend or flirting with someone else only to make your partner jealous

Envy is incredibly difficult. That sly feeling is completely reasonable when you're at the moment, but it's not worth sacrificing a decent relationship. Practice how to relinquish any hang-ups and construct trust in a companionship.

3. Demanding access to personal electronic devices

One indication that you are insecure in that marriage is your tendency to access your spouse's electronic gadgets, such as mobile phones, laptops, or social media pages. You may be paranoiac, wondering if your partner has been engaging in inappropriate conversations online, so you feel you should be keeping her under check thinking that you're protecting your relationship by doing so.

This feels a bit frightening at first, but to realize that you can't change your partner's behavior by monitoring them like a security officer will give you a sense of peace. At the end of the day, its either you trust your partner, or you don't.

4. You're always monitoring social media

Even if you have the passwords for your partner's e-mail or the unlock code to her smartphone, the insecurities you have will still show forth. Rather than going straight to your partner's phone, you're obsessively monitoring her social media. You can even google the name of your partner or search her exes via social media constantly. That can result in irrational arguments and deeper insecurity.

Social media is a prolific killer of relationships, and the ease with which infidelity can occur over networking sites is amazing. The American Academy of Matrimonial Lawyers estimates that the word "Facebook" occurs in the filings of one-third of divorce cases in the USA. According to a survey carried out by Divorce-Online UK, nearly one in three divorces was the result of social media disputes.

That said, being consumed on the pictures of your friend by a new 'like' or being keenly aware of someone who is having conversations with them is not a real way of living.

5. Paranoia and uncertainty as to where your partner is

Continually checking your partner's location and motives can be tiresome for both sides and could undermine your relationship. Sadly, the hardest thing to do when you're insecure is to trust your partner. The next time you get into an argument with your companion over her true whereabouts, try to tell yourself that if your partner has never given you a reason to question her, you should stop doing so. It is one of the signs of an insecure man in marriage. Insecure husbands tend to exhibit this action rather than the wives.

6. Need for constant reassurance

You love me, huh? Do you really want to be here with me? Are you going to be faithful? Why do you still like me?

These questions are all motivated by insecurities. If you are unsure about yourself, you may find out that you are constantly requesting your spouse's reassurance for validation.

Unnecessary reassurance-seeking by a spouse is a sign of depression triggered by relationship anxiety. Even though some measure of your partner's reassurance is supposed to make you feel unique about your relationship, it should not dominate your conversations. If you feel stressed or need constant reassurance, therapy can be considered a great way of getting to know yourself better and learning to enjoy who you are.

7. You abhor being left alone

When you're insecure in your relationship, your worst fear is being left alone. The silence lurks. You'd like to be anywhere but left to wonder. This fear of being alone may also lead you to remain in an abusive relationship which does not warrant your time or attention. Seek advice or trust a friend or family member who can give you an external viewpoint about why it's better to be alone and learn to value yourself, rather than remaining in a bad relationship.

8. You fear confrontation

You might avoid conflict like a plague when you are dealing with insecurity in your relationship even when it is justified. This is because you're afraid that with the slightest sign of opposition, your partner will leave you. It is important that you practice truthful communication if you want to maintain a healthy relationship. This includes bringing difficult subjects out in the open and sharing one another's opinions and feelings.

If you are constantly suspicious of your partner and feel the need to gather details about their whereabouts with questions such as "How long have you been away?" or "So, with whom were you?" it's a strong indication that your relationship is unstable. Work with your partner to develop trust and establish goals that revolve around getting to know yourself better. Your partner just can't take away your insecurities, which is your personal responsibility

Overcoming relationship anxiety is a solitary fight. If you want to know, how to conquer anxiety or insecurity in a relationship, you must have power over your own self. But if you think that you really don't know how to avoid becoming insecure in a relationship and how to conquer insecurity in a relationship, search for external support. A therapist can guide you on how to manage vulnerability in a relationship. In order to understand how insecurities can be resolved in a relationship, it is important to figure out what triggers insecurity. Only then can you learn how to become safe and fulfilled in a relationship.

If you're thinking: "Why am I so uncomfortable in my relationship?" and you can't work it out on your own, please seek support. You would never be able to have a stable and satisfying relationship without the knowledge of how to deal with confidence problems and insecurities. Paranoia in a relationship can really drive a wedge between a couple. Signs of insecurity in a woman or a man need to be spotted very early in order to save the relationship.

HOW TO RECOGNIZE INSECURITIES

Knowing the driving forces that affect your actions and those of others is an important part of your life. Humans suffer from insecurities (self-doubt, loss of trust or assurance) that have a significant effect on their actions. The willingness to understand your own and other people's insecurities will potentially support you, in whatever circumstance or relationship you find yourself. Recognition is the first step in achieving change. This section will increase your awareness concerning insecurities, which will inspire your efforts to change and understand others better.

OBSERVING YOURSELF

Evaluate your own self-talk. Should you pay heed to the endless debate going on in your own mind? Self-talk is either constructive and optimistic or pessimistic and harmful to your well-being. Focusing on your self-determined negative characteristics will trap you in a state of confusion. Harshly judging yourself is not healthy for anybody.

Don't be involved in trying to judge yourself unfairly because it creates an unjust image of you. Giving up on yourself is harmful to your attitude, inspiration and outlook on life. Look in the mirror every morning and remind yourself about three things you like about yourself. The more optimistic you are, the more likely you are to gain trust and hush up your insecure self-talk.

Your negative self-talk can make it difficult for you to speak for yourself. Good self-talk should create the confidence to advocate for yourself.

ADDRESSING SOCIAL PROBLEMS

There are certain social situations that trigger anxiety and insecurity in people. Perhaps you're struggling to mingle at events, chat to others or walk down the school's main hall. Often people may feel insecure when they don't feel confident or well versed in a typical skill. The good news is that you can learn how to recognize and solve those problems.

Social circumstances can cause thoughts and emotions that at the right moment, you're not doing the right thing because you don't want to be humiliated. Use visualization strategies to calm down. Visualize yourself as relaxed only watching and enjoying the experience.

Seek medical assistance for social anxiety, which can help you analyze and question the feelings that misrepresent the truth of the situation and help develop healthy self-esteem.

In social situations, your insecurities can manifest as bullying behaviors. It is an attempt to manage circumstances, so you don't feel uncomfortable. Consider other ways to make your life a success, such as working with others, rather than imposing your own viewpoint on them.

Note if you feel awkward voicing your expectations and wishes to others, which may result in anger and resentment. When you only passively communicate your needs, your needs are likely to go unmet and you will start feeling rage and disdain.

Using assertive language to demand what you need. At first, it will feel awkward, but eventually, as your needs begin to be articulated, you will feel more comfortable. A fear of losing protection can cause negative behavior. For example, you might feel worried about the uncertainty of your safety if you get nervous, anxious and lash out at people when you get ready to travel.

ASK OTHERS FOR FEEDBACK

There are moments when it's useful to ask others about their thoughts. You cannot always know how you act so it can be helpful to get feedback from trusted friends or family. They can find that, in certain cases, you are incredibly quiet around other people, or freeze and shut down.

Not everybody can provide positive input, so find a friend or family member who can be frank with you without being rude, disrespectful or demeaning.

Ask the person if they think you are showing some insecurity. Request that they be genuinely honest.

When asking others for feedback about you as a person, you may feel insecure but your goal is to know more about yourself so you can alleviate your insecurities.

An example of positive feedback would be something like: "You seem to be very worried about fitting in with people you think are cool, so when they're around, you get really loud and out of control. I think you're awesome and have a lot to give to others and you should focus on improving your self-confidence." An example of negative feedback would be: "You're a complete weirdo and a slob." You may note that your responses are inflamed in times of upheaval and that you feel defensive. You can feel embarrassed and humiliated, too. Your behavior can differ from situation to situation, or in the presence of some people. Conflict, in many men, brings out the worst.

For example, you may feel insecure about your education, because when you were in elementary school you had difficulty reading, and, as an adult, someone makes a joke about what was said on a memo that you missed. You react to the individual with frustration, because his joke caused an embarrassment about your ability to read.

Think of some of the bigger disagreements you've had. Seek to find out what caused your reaction. Your response may seem out of proportion to what has been said. Typically, the underlying feelings that have been aroused may be linked to insecurity.

SURVEYING OTHERS

Kindly note the private circumstances. People usually act differently in private than in public. You may see more transparent, franker, or even more outrageous in your conduct in a private setting. People can feel more relaxed in private. It is good to see signs of vulnerability as it can lead to a more positive view of others.

Search for characteristics and actions such as envy (hostility towards another and presumption towards misconduct to another); selfishness (excessively centered on one's own desires and no concern for others); sulking (win power by moodiness).

If you want to explore the insecurities of an individual, be mindful that this is a sensitive topic. The person could reject a direct question like, "Are you uncertain about my sister spending time with me? Try to do anything like that," I am so thankful to spend time with my dad. I always feel supported by her, who allows me to be a happier person all around, which helps us." Whether you're in a community of friends, going out of town, or starting a running club lately, you can recognize people's insecurities by watching and engaging. It may be hard to convey and converse with an individual who has a ton of weaknesses. There are a few different ways of open demonstration of powerlessness.

Look for characteristics and habits such as excessive people-pleasing (attempts to appease others to stop being displeased); pride (an exaggerated opinion of oneself and boasting about all achievements); extreme competition (turns any circumstance or interaction into one that needs to be won); unnecessarily materialistic (surrounds oneself with costly things to persuade everyone that they are important).

Observe the vocabulary of the body as another means to recognize insecurities. A person who is unsure is going to keep his body in a slumping, distancing way as if he were trying to hide from the world. The same will be true of anyone who is optimistic. He will stand upright and straight and make strong eye contact with others.

STOP TELLING OTHERS ABOUT INSECURITIES

Take the individual away for a private chat. The person may not be conscious that he is displaying such behaviors. Let him know that his conduct is causing unnecessary chaos by saying, "Hey, I know this may be a delicate topic, but when you get too aggressive, it's disturbing a lot of people. I didn't know if you were sure of that."

ANALYZE INTERPERSONAL REACTIONS DURING CONFRONTATION

Watching people becoming defensive or frustrated may be hard to observe. It is also painful to be part of these disputes. If a person is put in a situation where he feels he must protect himself, he will reveal his insecurities by his reactions. Monitor carefully and you should have a clearer view of the guy and his motivations.

Check for characteristics and attitudes such as intense authoritarianism (know-it-all who are manipulating and bossing people around); defensiveness (cannot tolerate criticism without treating it as an attack); excessively passive (don't strike back or stand up for themselves).

When analyzing a confrontation, ask yourself the following questions: if the person gets angry, does he return to physical abuse? (Report this to the authority at all times). Does the individual say nothing or consent to have a passive-aggressive response (indirect resistance to your appeal, such as procrastination)? When he doesn't feel well about himself because he's lost his work, does he have a bad temper, seems irritable, and doesn't appear to worry about other things?

Analyze verbal reactions during confrontation. There are examples of emotional responses triggered by inherent insecurities. Understanding these principles is no justification for bad actions. Alternatively, require empathy so that you can feel safe, withdraw yourself from the situation, or settle the problem once and for all.

Ask yourself the following questions when discussing the verbal dimensions of the conflict: when questioned, does the individual target your vulnerabilities or call you names? Does that person answer with, "Are you calling me stupid?" when you say nothing about the intelligence of the person? Will he say things that are not said and distort words into an assault on himself?

EVALUATING RELATIONSHIPS

Observe the circumstances in private. People usually conduct themselves differently in private than in public. In a private setting, you might see more transparent, frank or even ridiculous behavior. In private, people maybe feel more relaxed. Detecting signs of vulnerability is important, as it can lead to a more compassionate view of others.

Look for characteristics and actions such as envy (conscious of others and suspecting others of wrongdoing); egotism (overly concentrated on one's own needs with no concern for others); sulking (control gained by moodiness fits).

If you want to address the insecurities of a person, be mindful because it is a sensitive topic. The person concerned can deny a direct question like, "Are you insecure about the time my sister spends with me?" Think of saying something like "I am so happy to spend time with my dad. I always feel helped by her, which allows me to be a better person all around." If you're in a group of friends, going out of town or joining a running club recently, watching and communicating can recognize people's insecurities. It can be hard to communicate and relate to a person who has many insecurities.

STUDY PUBLIC DISPLAYS

Look for traits and behaviors such as excessive people-pleasing (attempts to satisfy others to avoid being disliked); pride (an exaggerated image of oneself and boasts of all achievements); excessive competition (turns any circumstance or interaction into something to be won); excessively materialistic (surrounds itself with costly things to persuade others that they are important).

Observe the language of the body, as another means of recognizing insecurities. An insecure person will keep his body in a slumping, hunching way, as if he were trying to hide from the world. To anyone who is confident the opposite will be accurate. With his shoulders back, he will stand erect and upright, and make clear eye contact with others.

Don't ask others openly about their insecurities. Pull the individual aside to have a private conversation. The individual may not be aware that he exhibits these behaviors. Let him know that his actions trigger unnecessary confusion by saying, "Hey, I know this might be a sensitive subject, but it seems like when you are too competitive it upsets a lot of people. I didn't know if you understood that." Analyze behavioral reactions in conflict. It can be difficult to watch seeing others becoming defensive or upset. Being part of these disputes is daunting too. If a person is placed in a situation where he feels he must protect himself, his reactions will show you his insecurities. Watch closely and you'll understand the guy and his motives better.

Look for characteristics and actions such as intense authoritarian (know-it-all who bully and boss people around); defensiveness (cannot tolerate criticism without perceiving it as an attack); extremely passive (can't fight back or stick to it). When analyzing a dispute, ask yourself the following questions: Does the individual resort to physical violence if he gets defensive? (Inform the authorities also of that). Does the individual say nothing or consent to have a passive-aggressive reaction (an indirect resistance to your question, like procrastinating) then? If, because he has lost his job, he doesn't feel good about himself, does he have a short temper, is irritable and doesn't seem to care about most things?

Analyze verbal reactions in times of confrontation. Examples of verbal responses resulting from underlying insecurities occur. Understanding these principles is not an excuse for negative behavior. Instead, allow it to provide clarity so that you can remain secure, get rid of the problem or settle the dispute once and for all.

When analyzing the verbal dimensions of conflict, ask yourself the following questions: when questioned, does the individual target your shortcomings or call you names? The person responds with, "Do you just call me stupid?" Though you actually said nothing in relation to the intelligence of that person? Hearing things that aren't written and turning words into an assault on itself.

103

HOW TO DEAL WITH AN INSECURE PERSON

Dealing with someone who is insecure requires being compassionate, polite, and encouraging. Insecure people may have poor self-esteem or feel affected by their past. By giving them encouragement, you will assist them in reflecting on the positive and boost their self-esteem.

SETTING SIMPLE BOUNDARIES

Build interaction boundaries. People battling insecurity will need continuous reassurance and encouragement, which you may not always be able to provide. Speak about boundaries with them so you do not feel overwhelmed or irritated by their conduct.

If you're in a relationship with someone who's insecure, for example, they may want to know what you're doing and your location. Although it's important to check in with them over the phone or email, when you're out or away from them, speak to them in advance about boundaries. Stick to what both of you agree.

You may have a friend or student, who seems to need your constant attention. Defines good times for the talk and contact. Try saying something like, "I want to be open to you, but I also have some work to do. Why don't we chat after class or during lunch?" Assist to refocus their insecurity towards positive things. Insecure people also have anxiety about something or someone. Old boyfriends may have hurt them. Perhaps they were teased about their looks. Help lessen their anxiety and concentrate on positive thoughts.

Act as a reminder when they begin to dwell on the negative and seek to turn their attention to issues that are good. For example, "I know these people can be rude, but remember that you have my support and your friends' support." If the conversation seems to be focused on the negative, refocus the conversation on something good that you see in them or a neutral subject. Consider giving them a compliment on something. Or address issues related to shared interests such as films, sports or other events.

Stop spending so much time to drain people emotionally. Insecure people can drain emotionally, and then tend to make you feel more tired. With all their needs they will act dependent on you. Avoid feeling like their caretaker and set limits. Motivate them to come up with ways to cope without you always being there.

Set different hours when you are going to be talking and meeting. Instead of avoiding them completely, make sure that you set times that work for you. Be honest and respectful in saying you need some space, but that doesn't mean you don't care about them. Explain to them how often personal space or time away from one another can be safe.

Remind them that it is not exclusively your duty to make them feel better. To one person this is too much. Not only is this emotionally draining, but you might unintentionally cause them to rely on you 24/7.

Explore trust problems with a jealous partner. You will have a friend or a relative who seems to be behaving jealously and dangerous. They can seem to be behaving irrationally or in fear that you will be leaving them. Offer reassurance and identify ways to maintain a healthy relationship. If a jealous person comes forward with allegations, offer reassurance instead of getting angry.

Demonstrate how you intend to remain loyal and faithful, but that it has to be based on trust for the relationship to succeed. Explore any previous problems your partner has had with feeling excluded, hated or lied to by former friends, relatives or partners.

Encourage a feeling of self-reliance in your partner. Find ways to encourage them to have an independent life instead of sticking to yours. Help them find personal goals that will satisfy them.

Take control of your emotions. Recognize when people who are insecure begin to you feel nervous, angry, sad or irritated. When you feel reluctant to speak to or support someone who feels vulnerable, then take a step back and consider what would be best for you. If you feel like they stress you out, kindly tell them you need to speak to them later, and then expect to have a better conversation.

Take a break from something that's bothering you, or whatever. It can be as easy as taking a few minutes or more of a physical distance from the situation before you feel calmer. Try to say something like, "I know you're nervous, and I'm here for you. I need to take a break right now to unwind a bit. I'll be able to help you in an hour again."

PROVIDE REASSURANCE AND COMPASSION

Show that you take care of your words and actions. Demonstrate that, in a genuine way, you are emotionally linked to their feelings and uncertainties.

Say things like, "Just know I'm here for you and I care about you" or, "I know you can overcome what you're facing. You're a strong person." If this person is a close friend, family member, or partner, consider giving hugs or other forms of affection as appropriate. Just hug them when you ask them first, and if they're open to this.

Tell them it's going to be all right, and things are going to get better. Provide hope and motivation to succeed rather than reminding them of bad things.

BOOSTING THEIR SELF-ESTEEM

Allow them to fight with their own self-esteem. While you should try to support the confidence of the person with praises and by being a decent partner, the individual may in any case need to do some examination to improve their confidence. Try to motivate your companion to concentrate on their confidence by giving recommendations of what has worked for you.

For example, you could motivate your friend to seek for self-assertion on a regular basis to suggest things like, "When I'm having a bad day or feeling low, I like to improve myself with mirror compliments. I start by staring at myself in a mirror and then I choose one positive comment to say to myself, like, 'My hair looks really bright and shiny today! I love it!'"

See how insecurity impacts themselves and others. Insecurities can show in a number of unhealthful ways. Sometimes people are acting rudely, jealously, or controlling. Some individuals may lose understanding of whether their conduct is harmful to themselves or others. Seek to understand how insecure people are influencing you and others in these ways:

- **Relationship.** Do you feel that your partner is too demanding, dependent, controlling or not trustworthy? Help them become less reliant and trust worthier.

- **Work.** Do you find out that your colleagues are dishonest, disrespectful, or jealous of you? Help them do good stuff in the workplace and to be nice.

- **Family and Home.** Do you believe like your family or friends are judgmental, cynical, disrespectful to others, or chronically depressed? Attempt to deal positively with this at home by being a role model.

- **Focus on the positive side.** Insecure people often concentrate even more on the negative aspects of their lives, such as lack of affection, care, income, or recognition. They look like they've been exploited (and maybe they've been in the past). Give them any good stuff to reflect on.

- **Keep interactions light and optimistic.** Stop subjects that might lead to a venting session or more negative talk.

- **Remind them of things that are encouraging or inspiring.** It may be a good quote, a pet snap, pictures of family or friends, or other items that raise their spirits.

- Often, you can just tell them that you like their tops, accessories, a bow on their pockets, or a new gadget they're wearing. Tell them to feel confident for themselves.

- **Communicate with them about what they're doing right.** Support and improve their self-esteem by concentrating on things they're doing right, rather than reminding them of negative things. It is important for insecure individuals to believe that they have importance and respect.

- For starters, say things like, "That meal you made was wonderful" or, "You seem to know a lot about baseball" or, "You're such a great artist."

Let them know you appreciate the little things they do well. Their common and routine activities can always be ignored, so a reminder that they are doing things well can be comforting. For example, "Thanks for helping me understand the math issue" or "Thanks for giving me a ride" or "You're so organized with your calendar." Insecure people can feel like everyone is against them, or that they have nothing to give. Help them find those things they enjoy. Encourage them not only to go along with others but to discover items that are especially important to them. Consider events such as intramural sports, fitness classes or social clubs or music classes, volunteering for various non-profits or other organizations, etc.

Getting Help

Determine if their attitude or behavior is getting worse. If the person appears to be increasingly frustrated, distressed, irritable, or nervous for a few weeks, consider exploring ways to support their job, education, or family.

If at school, speak to a parent, school counselor, or psychiatrist about changes in their actions. If you are at work, speak to your boss or friend about whether they can provide additional support. If you're at home, talk to other relatives or friends for advice.

Encourage them to have a talk with a psychologist. Insecure people may believe they have a small support network, or they may not trust anyone around them. They may have trouble coping, and instead they may use unhealthy ways to cope. Approach them by referring to a psychologist as a way to cope with what's bothering them.

Note that psychologists are non-judgmental, and they always focus on providing help and healing.

Help them find counseling through their school, community, or place of worship. See whether there are support networks available, depending on the topic or the challenge they face.

Identify the other available resources to aid them. Let them know that they're not alone. Show them that people are interested in them. Encourage them to have more interaction with helpful people in their lives.

Approach them with optimism and helpfulness. Discuss with those supportive people that more help is needed for those who feel insecure.

Let them focus on the ways they feel included. Motivate them to do different, new things. Seek people with whom they can go, so they feel less lonely or nervous.

Identify ways within them to encourage freedom. They might feel like they couldn't do anything themselves. Teach them how to be more independent so they can feel more relaxed and less insecure. Stay optimistic and helpful in seeking ways to help deal with what's troubling them.

FIGHTING INSECURITY

Insecurity involves feeling inadequate or lacking in self-confidence. Most people have at one time or another experienced lack of confidence. While uncomfortable, the feeling is perfectly normal and very common. For some, these feelings are passing and do little or no harm; for others, insecurity can become overpowering and seriously affect their lives. It can stop a person from being truly themselves and prevent them from doing the things they enjoy. When you find yourself facing insecurity on a regular basis it may be time to make some improvements.

CHOOSE A POSITIVE MINDSET

Try to outline the root causes. It will be helpful to find out why you feel so to counter your anxiety. There is often more than one cause and no easy answer is possible. Take some time to reflect on your life, past as well as present. Make a list of moments that you have felt insecure. Identifying the things or people that make you feel insecure can help you identify ways to combat those feelings.

Consider such things as: did you suffer trauma? Crisis, right? A substantial loss? Is there a new situation in the past or a circumstance that has disturbed your everyday life? Examine your upbringing and your parent relationship. Were they supportive? Were they harsh on you or were they pushing you to succeed?

Try to decide what seems to cause insecurity — search for correlations between occasions when you felt anxious and what was going on in your life, and what other feelings you had. When do such emotions come up? Who are you? How is it you are doing?

Did you still feel nervous, for example, around your older sister? Also, are you feeling bad about your body after seeing magazines? Perhaps your fear arose from comparing yourself to others.

CHOOSING TO MOVE ON

Maybe you know there are things that have triggered your vulnerability in your history. Or, perhaps your fear originates from your current situation. Either way, you should move on from the past. Moving forward will help you surmount your insecurities. You might have or maybe have a coworker who continually puts you down. Take an intentional decision to stay away from such a person.

Tell the manager you want to work on another project or a separate team. If this isn't practical, tell yourself, "I'm going to ignore the negative things Tom says to me."

Change your attitude. You can't change the condition, sometimes. Perhaps you are still living in your hometown, for example, and you have a lot of bad memories associated with that location. But you can't transfer, because you have some important work that you are doing. It's time to look for a new mindset.

Remember optimism is a choice. Instead of feeling, "I'm never going to get out of here," try to suggest, "I'm going to love my new city a lot when I get to transfer sometime." For example, you might say, "I'm hopeful I'll be able to move to a new place I'm excited about someday."

Accept and love yourself. It can be tempting to be critical of yourself when you feel insecure; nevertheless, make an effort to support yourself just the way you are. Possibly you'll see that changing your attitude in this way will make a huge difference. Does your fear stem from the fact that you can't play football well? Learn to understand people can't be good at everything.

Say to yourself, "It's okay that soccer isn't my thing. I can still have fun cheering on my buddies!" Insecurity will get you feeling pretty down on yourself. Make it a point to celebrate your talents, instead of worrying about your shortcomings. Seek to make a list of all the wonderful qualities you possess.

Leave sticky notes around your house saying stuff like "I'm an honest and faithful person" or "I'm a very hard worker." Read one of the notes each time you have a negative thought about yourself. It could make you feel a little more optimistic.

When need be, seek medical assistance. If your depression interferes with your daily life, such as stopping you from performing routine tasks or communicating with others, then you may want to consider talking to a mental health professional. Find a cognitive-behavioral trainer (CBD), who can be especially helpful in resolving insecurities.

BOOSTING YOUR CERTAINTY

Be patient with yourself. One of the best ways of overcoming anxious feelings is to become an individual of greater confidence. It may sound daunting, but you're already well on your way once you've adjusted your mindset! Ensure that you relax and treat yourself the way you want others to treat you.

Everyone makes mistakes. It's a real-life experience. Seek not to be harsh on yourself when you fail to pick up the food you need for dinner. Alternatively, try to say, "It's not that big of a deal. I'm going to have a sandwich tonight, and make sure I remember the groceries tomorrow."

Get involve in self-care. Self-care involves making sure you meet all your needs. Sure, you know physical health care is important. Yet don't forget to always take the time to fulfill your emotional needs.

It also involves taking care of things such as bathing and personal hygiene, sleeping well, taking any medications, holding appointments, etc.

Allow time just for yourself. Choose an activity that will keep you comfortable. For starters, give yourself time each day to read a chapter of a novel. Or consider taking a bubble bath to relax.

Get moving. Physical exercise has proved to be a real booster for mood. Keeping into shape is a perfect way to gain trust. Seek ways to bring a little more excitement to your life.

Step forward. At lunchtime, go for a walk around the block. Attempt to go to the cinema, rather than walking.

Take one lesson. Learn to enjoy a different type of workout. Consider taking aerobics class or HIIT class at your nearest gym or studio.

Live assertive. If you feel nervous, you may have trouble standing up for yourself. Know your needs are just as important as other people's needs. Work on being more assertive and you're going to start feeling more confident. For instance, your older sister may make you feel uncomfortable with her put-downs. When she says the next time, "Don't let Linda be in charge of the party. She is a ghastly chef!" Talk up. You might say, "This year, I would love to host Thanksgiving. I really worked hard to become a better chef, and I think I'm getting better!" Set simple targets. You'll be much more in control when you have a strategy. In turn, you'll start feeling more comfortable. Take some time to set targets. You may cover long-term and short-term goals.

For example, a short-term goal could be: "I'm going to speak to at least two new people per week." A long-term goal might be, "I'm going to increase my job performance and I'm going to apply for a raise one year from now."

BUILDING SUPPORTED RELATIONSHIPS

Assess current relationships as they stand. Insecurities often come from within but are often put forward by others. Take some time to think about your existing relationships. Is there someone who puts you down constantly?

Think about your relationship with the parents, for example. Do you feel insecure, because they put you down constantly? Or perhaps your problems stem from the job. Do you have a coworker who will not accept your contributions to the team?

Surround yourself with those good thoughts. If you think your life includes negative people, look for ways to minimize your interaction with them. You're more likely to feel comfortable when you're around positive people.

If your brother is part of the problem, try limiting the interaction with him and concentrating on the supportive family members. You should tell your mom, "I'm sorry that next Saturday I won't be able to do a family picnic. But I would love to spend some time with you. May I take you, next week, to dinner?" Make your needs transparent. Positive relationships should get you feeling good about yourself. Communicate your desires to others, in order to strengthen your relationships. Such specifications may be emotional or logistical.

You might say to your friend, for example, "I need you to help me in my attempts to get in shape. Would you be a good workout partner for me?" Maybe it makes you feel bad that your husband is still late for the night of the date. Try to ask, "Sam, would you try to be on time for dinner Thursday? I want to know that date night is your priority." Creating a buffer between yourself and the people or circumstances that make you feel vulnerable can really be beneficial. Defining boundaries is a perfect way to ensure you have the emotional space you need. Create a list of those lines you want to draw.

For example, if your dad causes you any anxiety, you might set this boundary: "Instead of meeting Dad for dinner, I'll meet him for a quick coffee break. This way, I can set a specific time limit." Perhaps you're uncertain about your dancing skills. Create a bargain with yourself: attend the wedding of your friend but come up with a respectful way of declining invitations to reach the dance floor.

OVERCOMING INSECURITIES

We're both grappling with anxiety at some stage or another; it's a natural way to try to gauge whether our plans are going to be productive or end terribly for us. In the case of having to determine whether or not to climb a major canyon on a motorbike, this is a really good assessment. Yet being too inexperienced in real life to attempt even minor things, such as being honest with partners, limits your ability to enjoy the time you have on Earth. Life is always evolving, and everything that is secure today can be destroyed or gone tomorrow. So, if you make yourself stronger, you will still restore, conquer, and step on with your own will, and find joy everywhere you go.

ADJUSTING YOUR VIEW

Process to be realistic. If you feel like you can't do it, take a step out of yourself for a moment and pretend you're a totally different guy. Talk of what you're about to tell someone else about your case. For example, if you're worried about going to a party where you don't know a lot of people or you're interviewing for a new job, talk of the advice you'd give a person in a similar circumstance. When you look at it this way, you will find that there is little to be afraid of and that you will excel when you set your mind to it.

Write down your doubts, please. Write down all the stuff you're thinking about, and all the things that make you feel like you can't do it. Read them over and ask yourself how many of them are logical and how many are simply the result of cynical thought. Take the time to truly talk about what's at the heart of your fears — whether it's making a fool of yourself, deceiving your friends, or not getting the life you deserve. See how many of your concerns you can tackle, and how many constructive ideas you can dream about for all the issues you're worried about.

It's completely normal to be scared of disappointment or of looking terrible. From time to time, everybody has these worries. It's normal, though, to be so afraid that you feel like you can't do a single thing.

Remember all the success you've achieved. Instead of dwelling on all the moments you humiliated yourself, missed something, or simply looked dumb, you should take a long, hard look at all the moments you did pretty well. Think of the achievements you've had in college, the wonderful connections you've built, or all the occasional moments that you've made a group of people crack up because of your sense of humor. The more days you recall, the more confidence you may have that you will get more of them in the future. It might be useful to write down the wish of your achievements when they happen. Hold a log of accomplishment at your desk and fill it with proud successes and happy memories. When you are powerless to do something and are like you can't do something right, you can look at your list and know what an amazing, talented person you are.

Tell yourself, "What's the worst thing that could happen?" and be frank about your answer. If you have a new haircut and a few people don't like it, it's impossible to destroy the planet. When you really dislike it, so guess what——the hair regrows. Don't let these dumb fears deter you from doing anything new. When you know that the worst isn't that bad, you're more likely to be adventurous and take chances.

If you can't say when your comments stop being rational and start being crazy, try and run it by someone you know to be receptive to. They should be able to tell you whether or not the worst-case situation is realistic.

Now, ask yourself, "What's the best thing that might happen?" It's something dangerous people don't do nearly enough. Let's say you're worried about having a first date with someone you're matched up with. The best thing that can happen is that you and the person hit it off and continue a positive and fulfilling relationship. Isn't this worth going back on a second date? While the perfect thing is not necessarily going to happen, getting it on the table will help you handle new challenges with a good outlook.

Before you set out to try something different, you can always write down the best thing that can happen, or the top three things that can happen, and they're fresh on your head when the time comes.

REMEMBER YOUR POSITIV CHARACTERISTICS

To protect yourself, you have to keep your great qualities at the bleeding edge of your psyche. Create a list of all the things you enjoy about yourself, from your friendliness to your intellect, and keep it at the forefront of your mind while you interact with someone else. Insecure people prefer to concentrate more on the bad aspects of themselves, which causes them to feel uncomfortable with who they are.

When focusing only on the negative things that are different from yourself, you dwell on them and forget the positive qualities. If you've been harsh on yourself for a long time, it can be hard to think about anything worth it at all.

Practice positive self-talking. It's particularly hard to hear negative self-talk if you've been doing it for a long time. If you're constantly reminding yourself that you're a loser, a disappointment, or that you can't do something good, you're expected to feel that way forever. Instead, focus on reminding yourself good thoughts about yourself, and you're more able to tackle new challenges with a balanced attitude and a willingness to do better.

A good practice to make you feel confident with constructive self-talk and to reel in self-abuse is to tell yourself two really nice things about yourself with every bad one. They don't have to be connected to it.

For e.g., if you burn your tongue because you didn't wait long enough for your coffee to cool down and yell, "Idiot! That was a dumb mistake" to yourself, then you have to note, "But I play tennis pretty well, and I have a nice sense of humor." It might sound weird, but you're changing your attitude when you applaud yourself.

Ask why you say no to yourself. Start answering yes more often than not. Instead of asking yourself all the reasons that you want to say no to a new encounter, consider thinking over what could happen if you say yes. And if all of the responses aren't real, the yes situation might lead to new and unforeseen stuff. If you get a little injured when you say yes to a new experience, you will rebound and get a different experience under your belt than if you just said no. If nothing comes of it at all, you should be able to think that you are a kind of optimistic and outgoing person ready to try new things.

Say a distant friend of yours from your music class is contacting you and telling you they want to start a band, and they want you to join them. Your automatic response may be, "No way, I've never been to a band, and you certainly don't seem to know how to make a successful one — otherwise, I don't think of myself as a musician, and I don't have time with classes, and ..." In this way of thinking, before anything has gone anywhere, you've already shut yourself down and denied any exploration of the potential of the idea. You could get in contact with the friend and their families, have a fun opportunity out of it, and have a new story to share. Say yes to see where you're headed.

Unless you are uncertain about your relationship, try to follow any of the above steps. Often, seeking self-happiness is still going well. If you're a genuinely happier guy, odds are you're going to make certain people and your wife happier; that's why it's going to lead you to trust and away from fear.

TAKE ACTION

Keep nurturing friends. Notice your companions and their mentalities to others, to themselves and to you. If you continue to find that most of your friends are very negative, negative about clothes, appearance, actions, voice, or conduct on a regular basis, you will want to search for less judgmental friends. Rather, try to find people who have positive things to say about others and are not eager to pass judgment.

Though getting a few supportive friends is great, if you're overwhelmed by animosity, even though it isn't aimed toward you, you're experiencing the impact. Also, if your friend speaks negatively about someone else's crazy hairstyle, if you happen to like that hairstyle, you're feeling like you were wrong and losing faith in your own opinion.

Be more compassionate of others. Don't be quick to pass judgment on yourself. Trying to bring someone down may sound like it's bringing you up, but actually, any time you strike someone else down, you're just undermining the standard you have, and you're knocking yourself down, too. Instead, lift others. Not only are you going to have more luck making friends and establishing successful relationships, but you will also be elevating yourself.

If you consider yourself condemning the mistakes or actions of others, think about why you do so. In the event that your first response is "possibly, they're off-base," think somewhat more profound. How is this wrong? In what way, then? Was it your cultural history, or how you were born, it makes you think so?

Will someone with a different world or cultural context feel the same way? Even if everyone is doing something different from you or behaving in a way you wouldn't like, it doesn't necessarily make them wrong.

Do one thing that gets you happy every day. It doesn't have to be dangerous — just drive to a part of the city you've never been to on your own and head to a random shop. Imagine what you're going to find there. Please try talking to the clerk. The more thrilling new encounters you have, the more likely you are to be curious about life instead of scared of new events or unfamiliar situations. When you know that you're capable of doing amazing stuff every day, you'll stop believing that something you do will end up in disappointment.

If you're self-conscious about your appearance, try to go to a clothing store beyond the norm and wear a bunch of clothes that you know don't fit your tastes. You joke at your reflection in the mirror. In reality, you might find something that surprisingly suits you. If you don't, you've got your own comfortable clothing that may feel a bit less absurd right now. Only try the new stuff as much as you can!

Fix the vulnerabilities that you should find. When you hate the freckles or the tone of your own voice, there might not be anything much you can do about it. When you have shortcomings that you can't alter, you've got to focus on embracing them. So, if there are things that you can improve about yourself, such as how quickly you get stressed out, your lack of understanding, or your lack of belief, then you need to take several actions and focus on something that you can do. Sure, we're all born with a certain temperament and it's hard to change yourself fully, but you can certainly focus on enhancing the consistency that you do improve.

If you take steps to change stuff you don't like about yourself, in no time can you be on your way to feeling more comfortable.

Nobody said it was straightforward to find out what you want to do for yourself and just go for it. Yet that is better than the alternative: to bemoan all the stuff you don't like about yourself without raising a finger to do something about it.

AVOID COMPARING YOURSELF TO EVERYONE ELSE

Some of the easiest ways to say you're going to be unhealthy is to equate yourself with the people you meet, or even the ones you see on television. If you do so, you're bound to find a way to make yourself feel bad, weak, inadequate, or a variety of other unflattering things only because you feel like you will not measure up to anyone. Rather, concentrate on issues that will make your life easier under your own standards, not by someone else's. If you search hard enough, you will still be able to meet someone that is happier, smarter, and wiser than you are. Yet odds are, there are a lot of people who wish they were more like you in some respects, too. The grass is still greener, and the person you may think is amazing and has it all together may wish he or she were someone else.

TALK TO A TRUSTED FRIEND

One way to conquer the anxiety is to speak to a close friend about it. Finding someone who knows and respects you will help you develop an impartial view and make you believe like your worries or doubts are unfounded. A good friend is going to cheer you up, remind you that you will achieve your dreams, and help you dispel all of the disappointment and questions that accompany your life.

Even learning about it is half a fight to overcome it. You may feel bad because you've been putting your insecurities on the inside of you. Hard to win at anything like that. When you want to feel better for yourself, one way to do so is to be good at it. It may be dancing, writing short stories, drawing, telling jokes, or becoming a speaker of foreign languages. It doesn't matter what it is; what counts is that you have invested enough time and money on it so you can claim, "Yeah, I'm pretty good at this." Making an attempt to excel at something and having a promise to do so consistently will certainly make you feel positive about yourself.

To be sure, you're not meant to be the best basketball player on the field or the sharpest pupil in the math class to please anyone. You're expected to do it to make yourself happy.

Learn to laugh at yourself, man. In fact, people who are confused take themselves very seriously. They're just concerned about their own loss or humiliation. Someone who has a decent sense of humor about themselves and recognize that everyone's making a fool of themselves appear to be happier from time to time, so they accept that sometimes they're going to screw up and that they're cool with it. You should learn to laugh at yourself and make jokes if everything doesn't go as expected, instead of stressing about coming out looking nice all the time. It's going to be a huge relief to face the day with more fun and less concern about everything going smoothly.

That doesn't mean you're going to be completely self-deprecating and joke at your own expense all the time. That does mean that you will treat yourself more gently and with more forgiveness; once you joke with yourself, people will be more relaxed with you and they won't be afraid to hurt you all the time, so you'll find that you feel more comfortable with yourself in return.

LEARN AS MUCH DETAIL YOU CAN ABOUT IT

One reason you might feel uncomfortable is that you dislike coping with confusion. You may not know what to do at a wedding, in a college class, or on a trip where you don't meet a lot of people. While you can't predict what could happen in a particular situation, you can make yourself feel a little better by collecting more details about it so that you feel a bit more in control. It will make you more comfortable in what's going to happen.

If you're going to a party, try to figure out who's going to be there, what sort of stuff people are going to do, what the dress code is going to be, and so on, and you feel like you have a better idea of what to expect.

When you're thinking about making a talk, make sure you know how many guests there are, what the room is going to be like, who else is going to speak, and so on, so that there are fewer things you need to think about.

NOTE, YOU'RE NOT TRAPPED

You may feel like you are the only one in the world who is continually doubting himself or feeling like he doesn't measure up. Nonetheless, you have to note that at one time or another, everybody feels vulnerable, even supermodels or highly wealthy businessmen. Insecurity is just a fact of life, and once you stop feeling bad about your insecurity, you're always on your way to feeling better! Everybody has something that he or she is uncertain about, and the questions are completely natural. Understanding this will make you feel better on your journey.

Seek a reflective meditation. Stand back or lay down quietly with your eyes closed, concentrating only on your breathing for 10 minutes. Try to rid your mind of all emotions that trigger discomfort and relieve physical pain in your body.

Meditation will take your mind away from fear and anxiety, leaving you with a sense of peace and relaxation.

STOP BEING INSECURE AND LOVE YOURSELF

The more we get hooked to social media, and the more and more life appears to be wasted on expensive handbags and flashy cars and beautiful faces, sometimes it feels very difficult to love ourselves. We are confused of who we are and what we have to bring, because we cannot see that we are no better from everyone else. Nonetheless, protection can only be the incentive you need to become a better person. Take it and don't let it go – face it, embrace it, and you'll be on your way to self-acceptance and happiness.

ADJUST YOUR MINDSET

Distinguish between what is actual and what is imaginary. There are always two realities running parallel to each other at any given time: the one outside your mind and the one within your head. Often taking a look back is what you need to see that everything you concoct in your head has so little to do with reality. Instead, it's just the worries and anxieties that grab hold of you. When you feel nervous, remember: is this reality, or is it just my reality?

Let's presume that your boyfriend texted "Yes" back to you when you went on this big, shimmering, nostalgic spree about how wonderful your birthday is tomorrow night. You start saying, "Ohmigod. He doesn't matter. He doesn't matter for me. What am I doing? Is this it? Are we going to break up?" Woah. Stand up. Wake up. Will "OK" mean all of these things? Yes, yes. It is your mind running away from you. This may mean that he's tired or not in the mood, but it doesn't mean that things are over.

Individuals prefer to dwell on the bad and to see the worst of otherwise innocent circumstances. Trying to concentrate on what's already in your head will help you continue chipping away at your fear, which allows your crazy imagination to succeed.

Know that your protection is transparent to you. How about we assume you're heading off to a gathering where you know for all intents and purposes nobody, and you're totally apprehensive. You're feeling overly powerless, you're starting to question on the off chance that you've at any point come here, in light of the fact that you're certain everybody's gazing at you, so you can perceive how risky you are. No doubt, they can see that you're energized, however, that is it. No one can see the insides of you. Don't let the completely unseen drive you away from who you want to be.

Some of us are so wrapped up in the way that we believe that everyone knows how we feel and can sense that we are dangerous, making the situation even worse. Fortunately, that's just not real. No one is punishing you because you're confused, and no one can say.

You don't think everything is as it is. Have you heard about the lady who invented a trip around the world to include her dearest friends and family? Through Instagram, she's shared all these pictures about how amazing her holiday was when she was just stuck at home, faking. In other words, people just let you see what they want you to see – there's something far less enviable behind those curtains. Everything is as it seems, no one is as it appears, so there's no need to compare your lot against someone else's.

As Steve Furtick says, "The reason we're dealing with anxiety is that we're matching our behind-the-scenes with someone else's highlight reel." We're going to think about the similarities in a moment, but please remember that you're looking at someone's highlight reel, not the true body of their job.

EMBRACE YOUR FEELINGS

Another way to combat fear is actually not to consider it. Aside from the fact that this just squashes you before you blow up, it also gives you a warning that the way you feel isn't real or isn't accurate. When you're not all right with how you feel, you can't support yourself. if you can't embrace yourself, you're going to be confused. So, take the little emotions and enjoy them. They could go away until you do.

However, this does not mean that you accept your feelings as real. "I'm overweight and disgusting" is something you can encourage yourself to fear, not think. Recognize why you feel this way, and then you should remind yourself why and do something about it.

BOOST YOUR SELF-IMAGE

If you want to compare yourself to someone else, compare yourself to yourself. Perhaps, when you look at other men, you look at a highlight reel. Don't do it. From doing it when you hear yourself. Just pause it. Mind that this is the highlight reel you're recording, and the reel is pretty damn short.

So, if you have a comparative gap that needs to be filled, just compare it to you. How are you going to improve? Which kind of skills do you have today that you didn't have before? Why the heck are you a happier person? What did you learn? After all, in the race that's life, you're the best competition you've ever had.

List all of your positive qualities. It's alarming. Take a sheet of paper and a pen (or your phone) and write it down. What do you like about yourself, huh? Don't pause until you have at least five of them. Was that a talent? A physical trait, huh? A trait of personality?

If you can't think of someone (you're not alone), ask a couple of close friends or family members what they think are your strongest attributes. Besides, there are lots of studies that suggest that some know us better than we know ourselves.

If you are down for the count, take on an attitude of appreciation, and the doubts can only begin to fade away. Search online for self-assertion lists that may also be used if one cannot come up with good attributes.

Take care of your body, your room, your time. In order to love one another, our brains need to have some evidence that we did. When anyone treated you poorly, you wouldn't accept that they loved you, so that's the same thing about you. Here's what you need to hold in mind: take care of your body. Exercise, be well, get enough sleep, and maintain 100% as much as possible. That's the bare minimum.

TAKE CARE OF YOUR MIND

When you live in a mountain of potato chip boxes, you certainly won't be able to take on the planet. What's more, you do need to take care of your internal room. Do meditation, do yoga or find another way to keep the mind stress-free.

Please take care of your time. In other words, find room for A) chill, and B) do what you do. With these two things, joy is falling into line – a big barrier to self-acceptance.

Establish the limits. Let's hope you're doing you properly, and you know how to treat you, but what about the others? Define the limits – in other words, what are you and you not going to put up with? Who contradicts your definition of "Okay?" Why is that important? You have freedoms and you deserve to be treated the way you want to be treated. You just need to learn how you're going to be handled to get started.

A perfect example of that is how long you're going to wait on a late partner. You might make a rule that you're not going to wait longer than 30 minutes. If they're late, you're out of there. After all, your time is precious – you're precious. They're disrespecting you because they don't value that, and if they appreciate you, they're going to be on time.

If you're in trouble, show it. "Try it before you do it" isn't just an easily rhyming, trite bit of advice. Science really claims it functions. Also faking confidence convinces you that you are more secure, more knowledgeable, which can contribute to more incentives which improved results. If you need the extra dose of confidence, lean on your acting skills. Everybody is not going to be the wiser.

Don't know where to get started? Move into your body and deliberately release your tension-holding muscles. When we get stressed, we get physically tight. Letting your muscles go is a message to your subconscious and everyone around you that you're calm as a cucumber.

Chapter 10

CONFLICTS MANAGEMENT

HOW TO OVERCOME CONFLICTS IN RELATIONSHIPS

Relationship conflict is a conflict that arises either from personal disputes or from unpleasant emotional experiences involving two or more individuals. You may have a disagreement with your coworker, for example, because you have a really clean workspace and it's still dirty. This irritates you, and it creates friction in the box.

Conflict is part of any relationship. In any romantic relationship, where the stakes are high and emotions are strong, tension is inevitable. Conflict will, though, be worn on the surface of a relationship if it is constant, or if it blocks out intimacy, devotion, and encouragement. When you want to reduce tension in your relationship, concentrate on rising the positive rather than the negative. Look for a way to strengthen your relationship with your partner. Seek ways to show love and support yourself. Look for ways to create goodwill and confidence.

HOW CONFLICT IS DESTRUCTIVE

Conflict with your partner can make you feel assaulted or intimidated, helpless and powerless, and can cause you to withdraw. If something that your wife does annoy you, and you feel like you're under siege, you're less likely to react constructively, and you're more likely to return to old standbys like "silent treatment" that can eventually do more harm than good. Ultimately, that will cause the relationship to break down entirely.

When anyone asked you when you know how to settle the dispute, you would undoubtedly say yes, and if they asked you if silent punishment was a good way to deal with the problem, you would almost definitely say no. You know better than to succumb to these dumb tactics, but if you're upset enough, you do it anyway. Why? Why? Why fall back on destructive habits instead of actively trying to correct the relationship problems at hand?

EXAMINE YOUR FOCUS

When you are focused on protecting yourself from attack rather than solving the problem, a conflict becomes harmful. When focusing on the pain and suffering, you're making sure you're going to experience more of the same, because where the emphasis goes, energy flows, or as Tony says, "What we're always focusing on is exactly what we're going to experience in our lives." Tony will take a two-lane highway at 10–20-yard intervals only by power line posts. Most of these appeared to be roses, candles and images constantly decorating him. With so much room on either side of the post, it was surprising how many people reaching it had died or been injured. Why didn't the perpetrator get away with it? Why were they not swerving to either side?

This is because people should concentrate all their energy not to touch the stick. Nevertheless, our priority is setting our course. If we don't want to reach the pole, we have to focus on what we want to do: stay on the lane! By adjusting our attention, we can change the outcome.

This lesson discusses how you can save your relationship. When you concentrate on where you don't want your relationship to end, struggle and let frustration build up over, you'll find yourself where you don't want to be – either in a miserable, unfulfilling relationship or split completely from your partner. When you concentrate on dispute resolution and evolving together, you will get the results you expect.

COMMUNICATE

You have a short period of relaxation in a coffee shop. There are two couples seated near you in the store. The man to your left is debating with his wife about whether they want to go to dinner. He says, "It's never pleasant – you said so yourself last time." She responds, "Of course you'd say that, because they're my friends, and you've never offered a chance to any of my friends." He rolls his eyes, and says in a rather cynical tone, "We're here again. War and Peace, our own edition, volume whatever." They turn away and sit down in silence.

The individuals to your right are also thinking about how they want to have dinner with colleagues. He says, "I think I'm a little worried that it's going to go on for hours and that it may not be so fun. How are you thinking? She says, "That's what I get. I still want to go, but maybe we should schedule a time when we're going to have to make a compromise?" She goes on, squeezing his hand and smiling, "Plus, it's going to be good to get home early. "He smiles and nods and they keep reading and drinking their coffee.

These couples were faced with a conflict – in fact the very same conflict. Yet in one case, one knew how to settle the conflict and the other did not. One responded by relying on bad habits and using a gap between them to expand the conflict. The other has used the dispute as an opportunity to express their feelings and to improve their relationship. Which pair do you think will have a more fruitful and fulfilling union? Which marriage do you think will last longer? When it comes to how to save a relationship, Communication is at the top of the list.

TURN CONFLICT INTO OPPORTUNITY

In the example of a coffee shop, a couple found out how to overcome conflict in a relationship: don't get defensive; don't overemphasize your point; don't try to win an argument.

Conflicts give you and your partner the ability to agree with principles and results. They are chances of recognizing, appreciating and accepting differences. Place yourself in the position of your partner and seek to understand his or her perspective. Such interactions and emotions can be painful, but we will never develop if we only opt for comfort.

Conflict is also a chance to know more about your partner and to appreciate them even more. Learn to see disagreements as changes to something greater than as grounds for retreating. The next time you disagree with your partner and question how to save your relationship, try to see the good in the situation rather than the negative and resolve actively to work together for a more prosperous future.

USING HUMOR

The use of humor to break a thread of discussion is a successful tactic whenever you find yourself in a retaliatory spiral. Humor will relieve stress and encourage you and your partner to concentrate on what you really want – learning how to save your relationship – and not on what you don't want, another needless fight. If you sense an argument is escalating, take a moment to interrupt the debate. Crack a joke. Sing a song that will make your partner laugh. Make the dispute seem stupid.

Let's go back to the coffee shop example, to illustrate this point. You see the older set. Accidentally, the man spills his tea across the table and splashes on the favorite dress of his spouse. He gets up for some napkins and she laughs and comments at the other customers aloud, "He's been doing this to me for 20 years-never finished a cup yet!" Everyone smiles and the issue is soon forgotten.

Many people may have converted the situation into an argument, but this husband and wife embraced the moment by using humor to nip the retaliatory cycle in the bud and converted it into an opportunity to learn how to overcome tension in a relationship.

ASK THE RIGHT QUESTIONS

When you're wondering how to save a relationship, it's likely things went wrong for quite some time. Not only do you need to dig into the past to discover the true, deeper problems, but look to the future too. What it's about asking the right questions about yourself.

First, make sure that you start the exercise from the right mindset. The idea is not to criticize, dig up old grievances or remind your partner all the irritating things they do. You have to change your way of thinking to one of appreciation and acceptance. Take on the fact that life is happening for you, not to you. Also, the present state of your relationship gives you the ability to learn and develop – as long as you're open to what it has to teach you.

Now you're able to ask important questions about yourself: Why did your relationship break down? What are the limiting values that shaped your relationship, that you and your partner lived through? How can you live above them? Also, what do you both desire for the future? What should your relationship concentrate upon?

PRACTICE ACCEPTANCE

Apply your fresh positive mindset on your partner. Many of our partners will do things that hurt us or have specific behaviors you dislike. Note that no human being is flawless. Focus more on what they bring to the table, how they make you feel and the things you value and accept them instead of focusing on their negative characteristics or bad habits. You'll find that you'll soon start loving all the things that used to make you nuts because they're part of the whole person you love, your partner.

Remember the two in-café couples? The popular couple, who put effort into knowing each other's needs, reaffirmed their mutual support – they supported his need to leave at a certain hour, and they supported her need to socialize with friends. We consulted with each other, measured the needs of each other, and made it a fun problem to solve, rather than making anything small turn into a big argument.

Hear your friend and consider what they're saying and why they feel the way they're feeling. Also, accept yourself: be frank about your own emotions and feelings. Be your bona fide self. Personal failures shouldn't be the reason you're wondering how to save your relationship. Indeed they are a strong device to show your partner how much you love them.

BE AWARE OF YOUR NEGATIVE PATTERNS

A confrontation with your partner can make you feel insulted or threatened, helpless and fragile, and that can make you withdraw and recoil. If you feel like you are under siege, you are less likely to react constructively, and more likely to return to old standbys such as "the silent treatment," which actually does more harm than good. In the end, this will cause your relationship to completely break down.

If anyone asked you if you knew how to fix the conflict, you would probably say yes and if they asked you if the silent treatment was a good way to deal with conflict, you would almost definitely say no. You know better than resorting to such dumb tactics, but you do it anyway if you're hurt enough. Why? For what? Why return to negative habits instead of actively trying to address the communication problems at hand?

Break the cycle of aggression and give positive energy to the conflict. Do not become defensive; do not hammer your point; try not to win. Why would you have wanted to lose your friend, the one you love?

Break the cycle of aggression and send constructive energies to the conflict. Don't take the defensive; don't pound the point; don't try to defend. How would you want to lose your friend, the one you love?

FORGIVE

If you're thinking about how to salvage the relationship when the confidence has fallen, you're likely to feel furious, jealous, wounded, mistrustful, and a variety of other negative emotions. When you're the one who lost the faith, you feel bad and ashamed. You may also want to accuse your wife or excuse your actions. All spouses need to focus on reconciliation in this case.

You're not only going to wake up one day and feel good about pardoning your wife. Forgiveness is a matter of thought. It's a series of little acts – accepting faults, exercising total integrity and putting your partner first – that add up over time. Forgiveness is doing a job.

When you are a trust-breaking partner, you will take full responsibility. Be mindful of how badly you upset your partner and give them the support they deserve. Place the partner first, so don't slip into a trap of self-denial. If your faith is lost, take some space, but keep talking. Let your partner know what you need to restore your relationship. First of all, never give up on that.

MAKE TIME FOR TOUCH

It can be tough to feel affectionate when you're constantly arguing with your partner – when any single thing they do is bothering you. Yet you've got to find room for contact. It doesn't only mean sex – it also means cuddling on the sofa during a movie, stealing a morning kiss in front of work and holding hands for no reason at all.

There's an explanation why loving your partner makes you feel so good: cuddling, kissing, and even rubbing your hands, triggers the release of oxytocin, a "feel-good" hormone in your brain which helps you feel protected and secure. Oxytocin will lower the pain, help you relax, make you feel closer to your partner, and also lower your blood pressure. You get all the benefits of getting married and taking your partner's side.

Don't deny sexual intimacy – except though you're nuts – otherwise you might find yourself in a totally sexless union. If you really want to learn how to save your relationship, continue with your physical touch. Cuddling before bedtime. Place your hands on theirs when you're out for dinner. Sneak a hug when you're enjoying dinner. Sexual love is not the product of a good relationship – it produces a happier relationship.

Relationships aren't that easy. We are all people, and human beings make mistakes. We've got flaws. Occasionally, we just don't get through the job that we need to do, so we just let our relationships slip by the wayside. We start looking at ways to salvage a relationship, even though it may have been ignored for years. Yet note this: a lot of marriages are worth saving. You just need to be able to do some sort of work.

FOUR VALIDATED TIPS FOR SAFE RELATIONSHIP

Building and maintaining a relationship takes commitment for most married partners who have been together long enough to dissipate (just a little bit) the initial fairy tale rush of passion and desire, to realize that a stable partnership is a juggling act that involves all parties to indulge in constant giving and taking.

Many of the following tips don't feel like "rocket science" because they aren't. To be successful, so set aside all cynicism and seek these ideas:

BE APPRECIATIVE

No really, express your affection and gratitude on a regular basis and not just on holidays, birthdays and anytime you "want something." Feeling loved is a fundamental human desire, and often in the crazy scramble of our days, we forget that a quick "thank you" or a nice little present (for no particular reason at all) or just carving out a little extra time for each other will sweeten all the best.

KNOW HOW TO ARGUE WITH THAT

C'mon, only the happiest people can sometimes argue over something, and regardless of whether the problem is large or low, Whether you argue will make all the difference in the universe. You may disagree with a circumstance or subject; you do not belittle or threaten the viewpoints or beliefs of the other party. Done in the best way, you will disagree on critical topics and maintain a caring and respectful relationship.

COMMUNICATION IS ESSENTIAL

Couples who have the strongest marriages learn how to connect and take (or make) time to do so. Open channels of communication, where they can communicate their feelings, desires, worries, goals and more, help keep couples deeply engaged in each other's lives.

GET SOME FUN

Perhaps we get so caught up in a day-to-day routine that we just forget what first drew us to our partner and what fun we "used" to have. Take a fun break or maybe make the fun break a weekly habit.

Let's face it, we all want to be part of a stable relationship. It just feels good, and the optimistic emotions that such a relationship evokes help us with some of the most difficult parts of our lives.

Yet again, there's no getting around that...you've got to focus on something. A good relationship (personal OR work!) will be a fleeting UNLESS thing you put into your effort.

Just ask someone who has a safe, prosperous and caring relationship; it's worth it.

COMMUNICATING BETTER IN RELATIONSHIP

Communication is hard work. That's why it's the secret to a stable relationship. When you want to connect well in a relationship, so not only do you have to learn how to bring out your thoughts, but you have to be able to genuinely listen to your friend. If you want to learn how to connect effectively in a relationship, follow these steps.

MAKING ARGUMENT

Learn to know what you're talking about. We've seen jokes about purpose and actual dialogue — when she says "this" she actually means — or, "what she's really trying to tell you is..." Such jokes are amusing because of how much they're valid. Often, we want our spouse to grasp our hidden intentions, but it's not realistic or efficient to trust or rely on. Instead, specifically lay out your feelings.

When you make your point, provide clear explanations of what you say and make your comments more important. Don't simply say, "I feel like you haven't done your share of the house..." Then, say, "I've had to do the dishes every night for the last two weeks..." Talk softly enough to enable your spouse to hear you. Don't just confuse all your hurt thoughts, or he or she won't be able to understand your argument.

Note, there's no bonus for chatting for as long as you can. Reach all the important notes you want to reach, but don't just speak and chat until your partner is exhausted.

Directly setting forward your feelings removes anger and doubt over your motivations. Instead of proposing solutions to your boyfriend's plans to introduce you to a dance, tell him the truth: you simply don't want to see all those people after a rough week at work, followed by, "I'm sorry to say I'm just not in a party mood tonight." Use "I" or "you" phrases. Don't launch a fight by accusing your friend of making a mistake. When you say, "You still ..." or "You never..." then your partner's guard will be up, and he will be less likely to respond to your viewpoint. Instead, say something like, "I've found that..." or, "Lately, I've been feeling like..." Having a conversation based on your emotions can help your husband feel less like he's being humiliated and more like he's part of a constructive discussion.

Just stating, "Lately, I've been feeling a little overlooked" feels more conciliatory than "You've been neglecting me." While you're basically trying to mean the same thing by "I" remarks, this soft-blow presentation may render your partner less aggressive and more able to interact freely.

Hold it as cool as you can. While you may not be as smooth as a cucumber when you and your partner are in the midst of a tense conversation, the calmer you are, the easier it is for you to express your feelings. Also, if you get frustrated in the middle of a debate, or even livid until you address the topic, take a breath before you feel relaxed enough to continue a constructive discussion.

- Talk in a soft tone to express your thoughts.

- Don't speak to your friend about it. It is only going to make you more furious.

- Take a deep breath. Don't get hysteric in the middle of the debate.

Keep a supportive body language in place. Getting a supportive body language will help to set a constructive tone for the conversation. Look at your friend in the head and turn your body around. You should use your arms to make a gesture, but don't push them so quickly that you're going to get out of hand. Don't fold your arms over your eyes, or your partner will believe like you're too oblivious to what he has to say.

Don't fidget with the things around you, because that lets you get the nervous tension out of the way.

Produce the ideas with confidence. That doesn't mean you're going to have to head through the conversation like you're off to a company conference. Try not to walk into the house, shake your partner's hand, and put forth a defense for yourself. Rather, bolster the venture by being as certain as possible with the circumstance. Grin every now and then, talk delicately, and don't stop, pose such a large number of inquiries, or sound befuddled of what you need to state. At the point when your companion has inquiries regarding your devotion to your feelings, he won't pay attention to you the more relaxed you are, the less likely you are to be afraid or dismayed. It is going to help you articulate your thoughts.

Have a game plan before you get going. Don't just step into the fight when you least foresee it and start showing your partner the 15 things he or she did wrong. Also if you're frustrated or hurt for a number of reasons, it's crucial to concentrate on the key argument that you want to make, and to care about the result of the interaction that you want to achieve; if your whole aim is to make your friend feel guilty for what he or she has done, then you can talk more about that before you continue.

Part of the approach will be when to resolve the matter. Bringing up a logical statement at an untimely moment, such as at a family barbecue or in the midst of a big sports event on television, will make the entire case null and void.

Thought of the particular reasons you're going to use to explain your argument. Let's just assume that you want your partner to be a better listener. Do you think about two or three times when he didn't care and really hurt you? Don't bombard him or her with harsh feedback but use persuasive facts to get the support that you deserve.

Consider what your aim is — is to ask your partner that you have been upset, to bring about a big confrontation, and to find a solution that can make you all happier, or to explore ways you will cope with tension as a family. Holding your target in the back of your mind is going to help keep you on track.

LISTENING TO YOUR SPOUSE

Put yourself in the role of your spouse. Use the power of imagination to better grasp what your partner's viewpoint could be in a given situation. Be mindful that there may be variables you don't know about. As he or she talks, putting yourself in his shoes

142

may make you understand that your actions or the situation at hand can be upsetting for him. When you're mad or frustrated, it's hard to see past your side of the conflict, but this strategy will potentially help you achieve a quicker resolution.

Empathy will generally help you overcome a dilemma in your relationship. Emphasizing that you're trying to communicate by saying, "I know you need to be irritated because ..." or, "I know you've had a rough week at work ..." will make your spouse see that you're actually listening to their point of view as a context.

Putting yourself in your partner's position will help you justify your emotions and let him know that you understand his problems and respect his feelings.

Enable your partner the ability to work through internal conflict. While it's nice to be able to hash out all of your anger, sometimes your partner is always sorting out his emotions and feelings, and he wants more time to figure out his feelings for himself. Giving him time and space to think will keep him from rushing into the debate and doing something he regrets later on. There is a fine line between facilitating a dialogue and pressuring your friend until he's able to speak and share.

Only saying, "I'm here anytime you need to talk," will make your spouse feel like you're taking care of him.

Give him or her all your energy. Know the signs that your partner needs to speak to — and that this is urgent. If he or she needs to chat, you need to shut off the television, switch off your work, cover your phone, and do whatever you can to give your friend your full attention. If you're multi-tasking or irritated, he or she is likely to get even more frustrated. If you're still in the middle of something, wonder if you should only tie things up for a few minutes, and you're less distracted when the time comes.

Holding eye contact instead of looking around at other items that could capture your attention will also make your companion feel like you're actually listening.

Allow him or her end, then nod your head or say, "I understand how you feel," to remain linked from time to time.

Let him end that. While he could suggest something totally ridiculous or something you feel that you just ought to fix, don't step in and disturb him in the midst of expressing his thoughts and feelings. Make a mental note on every issue that you believe you need to discuss later but let your spouse say everything that he has to say. When it's over, it's going to be your turn, so you can dive through these points one by one, or opt to tackle them later, at a different moment.

This can sound nearly daunting because you feel like you just have to hop in and out and make a counter-argument, but your partner may feel much happier after he has it all off his chest.

Hold in mind the distance. If you listen to your friend, you will know that you don't have to acknowledge or appreciate everything that he has to say. No matter how compatible you are, how similar you are, and how consistent your priorities are, there will be moments when you simply don't see a scenario eye to eye, no matter how hard you all try to express your emotions. That's all right. – Being mindful of the difference between your perception of the situation and that of your husband will make you more open to what he has to say.

Being mindful of this disparity can make you feel less upset when you're not talking to each other.

CREATING A SOLID BASE

Maintain anonymity. That doesn't mean you're going to jump into bed with your wife every chance you get to make up after fighting. This means that you can be as comfortable as you can, whether that means cuddling, caressing each other and smiling over nothing, or simply sharing time on the sofa with your hands and enjoying your favorite television shows. Allow time for affection at least a couple days a week, no matter how busy you are — this can support you when the time comes to chat about the rough stuff.

Feeling relational has a more essential significance than being physical. It's about seeing someone else and wanting to create a space in your mind for your partner's words, body language, or acts.

Check to see if your spouse is angry. Yeah, it would be nice if your husband were to let you know that any time something important really bothered him. However, this is always the case. If you want to create a strong base for conversation, you need to begin to identify non-verbal or verbal signals that let you know that your partner is angry. Learn to know the symptoms of your husband and be confident asking, "Oh, you look upset. Is anything bothering you?" He may not necessarily want to chat, so making him mindful that you know he's frustrated will help him feel more respected.

Every individual can demonstrate that he is upset differently – that he remains clearly silent, that he is not happy, that he makes passive-aggressive remarks, or that he talks over something trivial when something big is actually on his mind.

That doesn't mean that you can ask, "Oh, what's wrong?" – He or she might be exhausted after a hard day at work. Recognizing the symptoms and understanding that your partner is not all right is different than telling him if he's all right on a regular basis. This could get irritating.

Often the language of the body may express better than individual words.

If you are stuck in a disagreement, it is necessary to develop your ability to communicate. They can dig into true emotions in a method equivalent to: "I'm trying to comprehend, but I'm not getting there. Am I doing anything to annoy them?" "No." "Are you really angry?" "Yes." "About me?" "No. Not necessarily." You're narrowing things down. It sounds like a lot of work, but it may be worth it in the end.

Be constructive here. You don't have to combat any single thing that worries you, but when the time comes, you will be able to handle the difficult problems. Don't get passive-aggressive and let your frustration simmer, or you'll find yourself having a full-blown fight at an untimely moment. Prepare to answer the big questions so that you can be comforted by seeking a solution, instead of causing yourself to churn at or past the boiling point.

The two partners of the partnership will propose options before you find one that is mutually agreeable. A genuine agreement is one in which all parties agree like their thoughts and concerns are being discussed while adhering to specific constraints: viability, time, expense, etc.

Lighten things up. Find time just to have fun. When you waste all your time working and then battling your issues, you're not going to enjoy your relationship. When you put a lot of points in your "good wallet" and have a lot of pleasant thoughts and experiences of your friend, you're less likely to erupt in the middle of the fight. Creating a strong base of shared affection and joy would bring you transcend tough times.

Laugh together, guy. If you're making corny jokes, enjoying a comedy, or simply cracking down on nothing, humor would always make you love the relationship more and brace for a tough time.

Realize that a discussion is no longer successful. When both of you yell, injure each other, and don't get anywhere, well, well, the talk is no longer constructive. There's no reason to keep struggling if you just make it worse. Then, take a breath, remind your friend that you should both slow down and strike up a topic at a later time. It is a smart way to keep the contact out of control.

Only say, "I think this problem is very important to all of us, so we will go back to it when we're all calmer and our minds are more resolved." Don't rush away by closing doors or saying hurtful stuff. Exit on a good note, even though you do feel furious.

Perhaps you could even disagree over nothing to get a response out of each other. If that is the case, please find that out. Ask, "Who are we fighting for?" It will help all of you take a look back and take stock of the situation.

Know how to negotiate. Being happy in any decent relationship will always be more critical than being right. Don't waste all your time trying to prove that you're right or struggling to get your way, or that your marriage is going to fizzle. Alternatively, try to find a successful compromise that will make you all fairly happy. This is much safer for your long-term relationship, and it will allow you to express your true needs. However, you really won't be able to get your way when it comes to a black-and-white issue, such as seeking a new place to stay. Also, make sure that there is a good balance between giving and taking.

Take turns now. One person isn't always meant to get his or her way.

Having a pros and cons list will also help you consider a solution that is more rational and less hot.

Often, when you have a disagreement, it's important to remember which person really matters. This will help you find out how to cope with the problem. If it's very important to you, so it's just sort of important to your friend, let it be known.

Try not to stop for a second to help each other. When you want to keep a positive flow of conversation running, so you and your partner need to take the time to show your gratitude for each other's recent acts, give each other nice messages, remind each other what you enjoy and make time to do the things you do. A monthly date night, and as many regular meals as you can afford, will also help you enjoy each other's business and get used to referring to each other in a meaningful way. That, in effect, will make it possible for you to have a positive argument when the time comes.

You should give your partner much more positive than negative feedback in any good relationship. Basically, if you feel like he's doing the right thing, let him know!

STEP BY STEP INSTRUCTIONS TO RESOLVE CONFLICTS IN YOUR RELATIONSHIPS

Any association in our lives – organizations, families, sentimental and proficient – might be destroyed by struggle. The arrangement isn't to maintain a strategic distance from the issue or move about in the desire for drawing in a gathering of better men. We have to manage the difficulties we're really having, else they're just going to return somewhere else.

In a noteworthy degree, the main thing we can change seeing someone is our own conduct and our own. We shouldn't request that others improve, so we should attempt to manage connections in a way that supports harmony and lessens strain. Settling issues seeing somebody is one of the most critical central capacities that we will build and the thing we need to respect.

SEEING THE CIRCUMSTANCE FROM THE PERSPECTIVE OF THE OTHER INDIVIDUAL:

in the event that we have a difficult inquiry, it is critical to think about the quandary from the perspective of the other individual. That kind of understanding will in any event permit one to consider where they originate from and why they have their own extraordinary perspective. On the off chance that we may do that, we can get a kick out of the chance to mollify our position so we welcome that they are carrying on in a specific way. When we look at it from our viewpoint, confrontation is much more likely to occur.

TOLERANCE:

The biggest source of tension in relationships is that we want individuals to act in a certain manner. The issue with anticipating any kind of activity is that we get disappointed when they neglect to satisfy our gauges. Indeed, even individuals who are near us are not our obligation; we should be conscious of their blunders and weaknesses. We should respect their decisions about how to live their lives. Such disconnection isn't lack of interest; we should keep up sympathy and appreciation, however, there is a phase that we have to permit individuals the option to settle on their own choices – despite the fact that we don't concur with them. This is especially valid for guardians who have a domineering vision of how their youngsters will live their lives.

MANAGING ANGER:

Sadly, in the event that we respond to issues by getting irritated, we will raise the issue. Outrage mirrors the feeling of threatening vibe and dismissal that individuals can't adapt to. It generally encourages individuals to respond along these lines. If we feel frustrated, the safest approach is to stop talking or arguing at the precise moment. Until addressing other people, we will cool our rage. Any dispute can only be exacerbated by frustration. Likewise, if people threaten us with frustration, we have to react in a different way — silence is better than getting angry at anyone.

PRICE HARMONY:

To a great degree, we're seeing what we're looking for. If we really organize harmony in our associations with others, at that point we're going to get that going. In the event that we allot more noteworthy accentuation to substantiating ourselves right and our own pride, at that point there will be a persevering feeling of strength and inadequacy which will offer ascent to struggle. At the point when we continue helping ourselves to remember the allure of harmony, we won't permit ourselves to get detestable and hopeless; we will make a solid effort to consider others.

UNITY:

The genuine mystery to safeguarding solid connections is to assemble a sentiment of unity. This implies we will be useful for the accomplishments of others; we will identify as they face troubles; we will look to quit hurting their emotions. There is no amazingness and inadequacy incongruity. Regardless of solidarity, we are helpless against sentiments of vanity, jealousy and dread. When you have a solid feeling of being unified with other men, how would you like to harm them?

UNCERTAINTY AND INTERNAL POISE:

If we are brimming with frailties, our fellowship gets increasingly convoluted. The problem is that since we are uncertain for ourselves, we will be censured by others; to cause ourselves to feel better, we can keep on accusing others. They may not know about that, yet it happens. Once we have harmony with ourselves, healthy relationships would be normal. We prefer to have a compassionate and optimistic view of the world while we are at ease with ourselves. Sometimes we try to blame other people for broken relationships; but, really, the only thing we ever can do is focus on ourselves. When we cultivate inner harmony and order, our relationships will certainly strengthen.

TALKING:

If stressful situations occur, conversation can be the most productive way to get through the question. Many issues are best kept unsaid; it is not advisable to dig up old disputes when they aren't completely necessary. When we chat, we will continue to think about constructive issues; look for stuff that we reflect about and should work on together.

PERSPECTIVE:

Don't get angry over the little things. Within the big interstellar war, the bulk of small personality differences are fairly meaningless. When we get angry when someone doesn't do the washing, how are we going to behave when they do something really bad? At the point when you wind up concentrated on an assortment of little issues, make a stride back and endeavor to decide their relative worth. For any minor that battles, attempt to consider the individual's general acceptable characteristics. If you are straightforward, you may accept that this high notoriety is significantly more significant than a minor carelessness.

DEVELOPING ISSUES:

While we would prefer not to uncover old appraisals, once in a while it's important to make every other person mindful of the issues they're making. In the event that we accept like another person is consistently accomplishing something incorrectly, we have to make them mindful of their activities in a non-fierce way. Numerous individuals truly don't understand the issues they're making, so they would truly appreciate being made mindful of the issue. The least difficult system is to attempt to make them aware of how their activities carry mischief to other people; however we have to attempt to do as such in a way that doesn't cause them to feel really awful. Give them time and permit them to make the suitable enhancements.

Chapter 11

YOU AND YOUR RELATIONSHIP

Having a partnership to last will often feel like a very difficult mission. Most of us are able to develop a relationship that lasts a lifetime, while others just don't manage to make things happen, despite being initially comfortable with each other.

THE LIFE CYCLE OF A RELATIONSHIP

Relationships tend to go through five levels – some are more satisfying than others. So if you and your partner are able to work together with each stage as they arrive, the incentives will be combined with development and a stronger relationship. However get caught in one of these stages, and you and your better half could simply wind up attempting to give up.

FALLING IN LOVE

Also called the "fixation period." It is the most glamorized period of the cycle of marriage. It's something that happens in the movies, and it's something that any of us care about!

Our own human nature causes us to fall in love with each other. According to Dr. Susan Campbell, our brains emit a bunch of hormones designed to make us feel attractive. Oxytocin, serotonin, and phenylethylamine (a stimulant of the nervous system, and a very hard word to pronounce) form a concoction that renders you as happy as heaven on fatty love.

A road trip just helps you to see the differences between you and your partner, as well as the qualities that make them a good person.

All this high blocks, you from seeing is their weaknesses, their shortcomings.

This doesn't always have to be a bad thing; we all have faults and characteristics that we'd prefer to keep to ourselves until we're more confident. Unless it wasn't for infatuation, we'd all be single!

After a time of growing up, our passion deepens and becomes relaxed with each other. Finally, we have a closer connection with our partner; we feel protected and treasured. A lot of people misinterpret that as the highest degree of affection we should have got, but they'd be mistaken.

Infatuated drug-love wears off – Campbell extends this wear-off from two months to two years – depending on the pair. Deepened passion continues a time after that, until the 3-4-year point of a relationship. Yet instead we're going to reach the risk zone.

THE REALITY CHECK

This is better known as "the love hangover" or "the disillusionment period." According to Dr. Campbell, an incredibly large number of marriages are taking place at this time. At this point, we begin to reflect on our weaknesses and shortcomings, rather than on the ways we are. The passion we have can be replaced by frustration and anger.

We can continue to get irritated with the little stuff more often than not. We will feel less cared about or loved than we used to do. Before this point, it was all right (though difficult to be parted) to let each other concentrate on work tasks – now, choosing work over each other feels like negligence.

At this point, we sometimes make the error of attempting to "transform" our partners by punishment: disagreement, violent conduct, and emotional isolation...the list goes on.

How can you work your way through this tough patch successfully? This stage is a time to reflect on your interactions – most importantly on the ability to settle disputes (see this post on how to argue effectively). Campbell's tips for getting through this point include:

- Acknowledging and appreciating your similarities

- Sharing control and knowing dominance won't get you what you want

- Recognizing that peace without conflict doesn't happen

- Embracing life because it is now time to remind yourself of your own personal shortcomings and failures, and to reflect on how your spouse makes up for them. Know what makes a team of you!

If you can't settle your differences successfully at this point, you can find yourself coming back to it regularly in your relationship. Some people have been trapped in this stage for years – never hitting the next point – until they stopped calling.

STABILITY

You've actually worked out how to compromise with – and not fight – your friend. Congratulations, you've made a hell of the past relationship, and passion is back! Phase one's older, smarter brother is the stabilization stage. At this point, you've embraced each other for who you are, and you don't want to change them anymore (you've never been able to do that anyway).

You have strong boundaries for each other at this point, as well as reciprocal respect. This love is true; it lasts. Today, with more faith than ever before, you can tell that you love each other completely for who you are.

Even in moments of disagreement or immaturity, it is understood that hurtful conduct is not due to either of you being cruel or uncaring. Yes, at times, you could struggle and have your differences. Yet this doesn't preclude you from maintaining a close bond with them.

At this point, however, some couples end their relationships. Stability can make certain people feel nervous or bored. Although it's normal to skip the thrilling infatuation of stage 1, some people are beginning to wonder if they can get that back with a new boyfriend. It may be the ignition that would set off an extramarital affair. Our advice, huh? Weigh what you've got to earn against what you've got to lose. Though falling in love can be fun and thrilling, it doesn't last forever.

COMMITMENT

At the point when you're intending to get hitched, this is the stage you're going to need to be in before you pose an inquiry. Couples now understand that while they needn't bother with one another (speedy updates that people will truly exist all alone), they need to be with one another, deficiencies or not.

Some people don't skip stage one; the only other way to get back to that is to meet someone new to marry, so they don't want anything else except their partner. Commitment is a real symbol of long-lasting devotion.

HAPPINESS

In the happiness point, people step past the inner workings of their partnership – they've got all packed up by now – and out into the world around them. Such couples prefer to collaborate on projects together. To certain couples, it means launching a company or a charity together. For some, this stage involves working together to grow up and sustain a family. Among these purposes, this period is most sometimes referred to as the period of co-creation.

Couples seem to spend a number of years at this point. Yet it's always important to note to carry on sustaining your relationship while spending this time and energy in their new passions!

Please note, these steps are not sequential, so happiness is not always an end goal. Numerous individuals experience these periods a few times in their relationships, months or years one after another.

This is crucial to have the option to perceive the phase at which you and your partner are in, so you can settle on more advantageous choices on whether to improve your relationship, instead of making somebody stage debilitate or fall apart.

OVERCOMING RELATIONSHIP ANXIETY

Relationship anxiety is an awful thing to experience. It means you can't enjoy the magic of being in love, so worried you are that your partner's going to fall out of it.

Ironically, all the negative energy you exude thinking about your relationship could be the reason your wife ends up wanting to end it.

Luckily, there's plenty you can do to relax your emotions and start re-adjusting your attitude so you can appreciate your relationship and not live in a perpetual state of anxiety.

Here are some easy ways to help you conquer your insecurity about relationships.

1. Know it's all going to be fine.

It can quickly feel like the end of the universe when you are in the midst of a relationship that is falling apart. With all of those emotions running about, putting things in perspective and seeing the light at the end of the tunnel can be incredibly hard.

However you need to know that whatever happens, all will be perfect. Just think back. You've already had heartbreak before, and you just got through it perfectly.

When you found your partner you were perfectly good and, difficult as it may be, life would start without them if things were ever going down

Even if your relationship goes down, your life won't stop and being in a relationship is not your key to heaven. A relationship may be amazing, but it never defines who you are

There is nothing you can do about it if someone doesn't want to be with you. If anxiety begins to increase, just whisper to yourself that everything is going to be perfect. When you convince yourself enough, you will continue to really believe it sooner or later.

The less you dread the end of the relationship, the more you can settle in and just enjoy it right now.

2. Talk to your partner about your feelings

A loss of contact or miscommunication is also a cause for insecurity about relationships, and it's important to be careful and communicate with your partner.

Speak to your partner from a position of authenticity and vulnerability if your partnership is more established but you still feel uncertain about its future.

Explain how you feel and tell them that your previous encounters are not the ones that trigger it. Seek to offer examples of scenarios you find difficult and how they can allay your fears.

If your partner is serious she will want to do what they can to give you peace of mind.

It can also allow them to communicate their emotions more compassionately when the fear forces you to do something that upsets them. They'll know you don't really mean what you're doing all the time so they can help you conquer your emotions by not adding more fuel to the flames.

The mere act of telling your companion about your anxiety will have you feeling better immediately. You'll feel like a huge weight is off your back and if they react kindly and lovingly, you'll be more assured they're not going away.

3. Nurture your independence.

If you're in love, you might feel like you'd be able to stay in the pocket of your partner if you could, but losing yourself in your relationship is a sure-fire way to increase your anxiety rate.

If you start describing yourself only in terms of your partnership, you are placing too much pressure on long term sustainability of the relationship. Above all, who would you be if you split?

Be sure that you do something for yourself intentionally and have a life apart from your family. Work to retain the qualities that make you special, which were undoubtedly the reason your partner was first drawn to you.

Your companion isn't the "other half" so they don't finish you off. You are just as fine and total as you are. It's great to be in a relationship but it's not important to your happiness.

4. Keep back from actively evaluating their every breath.

People don't think about every word they utter or examine the ways your nervous mind can perceive any text message they send. So, you shouldn't let the smallest things affect your mind.

5. Know you are the one controlling your mind; it is not your mind that is influencing you.

You've got the power to steer, shape and train your mind. You may still experience anxiety until you know it, but you will be able to recognize it for what it is and allow it to pass, rather than allow it to overtake you and control your behavior.

6. Avoid acting on your feelings

Sometimes feeling anxious about your relationship or your partner can make you want proof that everything is OK. Wanting to convince yourself is natural, but avoid the temptation of using this evidence in innocuous or unhelpful ways.

Be aware of the difference between your usual behaviors and your impulsive actions. Random text can be natural in your relationship and keeping a steady conversation can help to reinforce your sense of connection. Yet sending out multiple messages in an hour asking your partner where they are and what they do, when you know they're going out with friends, can lead to tension.

Attempt to calm yourself with some deep breaths, a stroll or jog or a short phone call to a close friend when you notice these urges.

Anxiety can be a threat to relationships. Even if a relationship, confronted with these doubts, continues unchanged, it will never grow to its full potential. Anxiety is an enemy whether it's in the relationship with your family, children, spouse or siblings. It's an enemy that must be defeated

CONCLUSION

In conclusion, I will be highlighting some ways to nurture your relationship and get the best out of your togetherness

COMMUNICATION

For most guys, this is completely strange, but without it, you will have a lot of problems. My girlfriend just called me for not explaining it much, and then went on to say, "You know; I just think you have a problem with communication. You never tell me what the hell is going on in your head. I'm not one thinking student. I sat down and talked about what he said, and I said, "When I tell you something important, I will always talk to you." Yes! Yes!

DISCUSS VULNERABILITIES

This one is related to the previous first point. Talk to your partner about things that might be a little difficult to discuss. Your feelings, your thoughts, what you have in mind, your worries, your doubts about the future and almost anything else that's edgy to express. It is a crucial channel for passion, affection and attachment, even if it does not seem like this until sharing.

SELF-AWARENESS

Self-awareness is the ability to examine yourself and recognize what you listen to, perceive and do at all times. This domain, the Jedi Masters will be able to have eaten exactly what is motivating their current feelings, words and deeds in their history. Having this self-awareness allows you to comply with the 2 partnership laws above (communication and vulnerability). Self-reflective activities that include: counseling, journaling and therapy.

EMOTIONAL INTIMACY

When you don't take care of your feelings, they will look for you. People who cannot or do not have access to their feelings will not be able to sustain a healthy romantic relationship. Time! The ability to recognize, connect and articulate your feelings safely will strengthen and enrich your relationship/life beyond measure. Feelings also send a very clear message about the world and what steps you will take to bring emotions back into balance.

HONESTY

Make sure you act honestly with yourself and your family. As far as I'm concerned, the concept of honesty includes understanding and harmony with your beliefs, behavior with strong moral maturity (in whose interests do you behave?), Keeping the promises you make in your life and aligning your feelings, words and actions. Ask yourself about your actions on a regular basis, "Is this the guy I want to be?" And "What kind of story do I want to leave behind?" Such questions are always enough to bring you closer to honesty. The environment that constantly takes men from self-confidence and their partners is sex. Release the sex, if you have one, and stop watching porn behind your partner's back. Porn and company are a convenient solution to get out of your family's problems.

TAKE RESPONSIBILITY

if you continue to blame others for problems, you will be trapped. Victim Mindset is a person who takes away your power and transfers responsibility for your life's problems to those around you. It takes two to tango, and much of the tension that occurs between two people is consistent with this metaphor. So stand back before you have your next point and ask yourself, "What do I add to this, and what can I do about it?"

SPACE BALANCING

Take up space when you need it, then make sure to get back in partnership when you're ready. The male essence craves only room and time but going fishing for the rest of our lives doesn't make us a better companion. It is essential that we respect the normal instinct to escape and calm down. Such daily bursts of time alone will give you an idea and encourage you to focus on some things on your own. When you do, go back to your family and share your new experiences with the people you care about.

TAKING A POSITION

At a young age, many people don't have the courage to speak for themselves. For example, being intimidated by a violent father or dictator will also result in the loss of his identity and his desire to defend himself and his limitations. Establishing and preserving the limits of relationships is important if you don't want to lose the sense of self for your spouse. Loss of trust leads to anger (from you to your partner) and loss of esteem (from your partner to you). Stay in touch with your inner indignation and using the strength and confidence that passion offers you to establish and preserve your boundaries. I don't want any of the threats.

RESILIENCE

Both partnerships require strength and resilience. It doesn't matter how happy you are, how much you love yourself. When you sign up for "Death do us part," it is best to buy yourself a helmet and dig for the difficult days ahead. Maybe you can look more like heavyweight boxers in the twelfth round of the title fight. It's completely natural and perfectly safe (as long as you're fighting clean)!

GET A MENTOR

This is and has been my first reaction every time I encounter an obstacle in my life that seems bigger than my ability to conquer it. Find the best specialist in the world in this particular area and read their books, organize a series of one on one matches and participate in all their seminars, etc. Don't just leave the knowledge you know as an abstract idea, apply it and turn it into a real reality.

Made in the USA
Coppell, TX
12 September 2020